THE FRAGILE MONUMENT— ON CONSERVATION AND MODERNITY

THORDIS ARRHENIUS

Artifice
books on architecture

CONTENTS

THE FRAGILE MONUMENT

Heritage objects today—monuments, city-quarters, regions, landscapes and natural habitats—comprise an ever-greater proportion of the physical environment. This increase can be understood both in terms of democratisation and consumption. Coupled to tourism, heritage has grown into an event industry of unparalleled scale and scope. On another level the 'past' today creates a strong force for social engagement that traverses contemporary society. Heritage and conservation now engage wide and diverse groups; the use and enactment of the 'past' takes on various expressions, from local preservation societies and grass-roots movements working to save heritage objects, to the re-enactment of historical events, to international cross-cultural campaigns for rescuing objects in danger.

This investment in heritage is extensive; the past appears as material for cultural production on a scale that can't be ignored. No longer just the obscured passion of the few, 'the old' is taken care of in an increasingly ambitious and widespread fashion. Every region, culture, or object now has its society or museum carefully protecting and documenting its specific touchstone. There is a quality of scaling in this development of heritage both as object and cult. In an inverted magnitude the monumental is discovered in the minute and insignificant at the same time as the generous notion of the monument miniaturises the large—whole cites, industrial sites and landscapes are framed in the name of memory and turned into heritage objects.

This book aims to understand the reasons and causes for this expansion of heritage specifically in relation to the built environment and architecture. To do so it argues that notions of conservation need to be analysed in terms that go beyond the validation of different practises of preservation to focus on the object that the discourse on heritage constructs, the thing we habitually call the monument.

In his seminal *L'architettura della città* from 1966 Aldo Rossi defined the monument as a "slow object". In the evolution of the city the very endurance of certain urban

Thomas Struth.
Notre Dame, Paris 2000.
Chromogenic print.

artefacts causes them to become identified as monuments: "A monument's persistence or permanence is a result of its capacity to constitute the city, its history and art, its being and memory", as Rossi beautifully writes.[1] While accepting the weight of Rossi's argument this book will argue the reverse; that it is not the permanence or the presence of an object that identifies it as a monument, but rather its very fragility and remoteness that singles it out.

Redundant from production, as a *lieu de mémoire* or a site of memory, to borrow a term from Pierre Nora, the monument is identified with a value no longer measured in terms of functional performance but in its ability to evoke what is lost.[2] Removed from the present for reasons of memory, history, and sentiment, this monument appears as a stranded object ready to authenticate the recovery of different pasts. The popularisation and expansion of the old in contemporary society appears to be closely bound to notions of loss and danger. Not until the object is threatened, homeless, on the edge of demise, does it qualify itself for protection and gain its status as a monument. Exposed and vulnerable, always in need of reinforced protection, this monument is at the same time both lost and found; at the point it looses its use-value it gains its memory-value.

Since its invention this, in one sense 'accidental', monument has been inscribed into a narrative of danger. Indeed, throughout the history of conservation various perils appear constantly to put its object at risk, and it is these different threats that motivate the whole series of actions—legal, physical or spatial—that conservation guarantees. This notion of danger has contributed to the formation of a discourse on conservation that, although framed as an issue of preservation, at closer inspection shows a strong interdependency between saving and destroying. The series of cases studied in this book, from the museum of the French Revolution to Le Corbusier's modernisation plan for Paris, can be read as a history of this interdependency.

It has been seen as a paradox that the transformative event that ushered in the modern period, the French Revolution, was accompanied both by extensive cultural destruction and, almost simultaneously, a new notion of conservation. In 1793 the *Commission des arts* was founded for the purpose of protecting historical monuments, and soon thereafter, as a direct result of the Revolution's expropriations, the *Musée des monuments français* was created to exhibit to the public fragments rescued from the vandalized city.[3] The new museum arranged its collection in a strict chronological order that curiously restored the monuments to their proper place in history. These monuments, when experienced as a part of Paris's urban context, had been variously juxtaposed; as fragments in the museum, on the other hand, their displacement in history was corrected. As pieces in the grand intellectual construction of national history, the fragments were made 'whole' through reading rather than through reconstruction; indeed within the scholarly frame of the museum the monuments in some sense reached a more complete stage than in their previous state as physically whole. The effect of the museum as a novel space of conservation will be discussed in the first chapter in relation to the terms "monument historique" and "vandaliste", both invented in order to come to terms with the Revolution's iconoclasm.

This interdependency between destruction and conservation continued to mark the discourse of conservation in the nineteenth century, which forms the context for the second chapter. The 1800s saw the establishment in most European countries of centrally organised commissions to manage and control the conservation of national heritage, endeavours that were often accompanied by tales of local mismanagement and of the destruction of national treasures in the provinces.[4] The emerging criticism of these state-controlled restorations was again based on arguments that the monument was at risk—this time not of falling down but rather of being too forcefully required to stand up; in their ambition to save monuments the restoration architects were charged with disfiguring them. The founding principles of restoration in the nineteenth century grew out of the restoration of Medieval buildings—mostly cathedrals and churches, buildings without 'authors' in the tradition of the architectural monograph; in the collective process of their making no individual had stamped the edifice with a signature and the prerogative of interpretation was open to the restorer, to recreate the building in a new and yet old shape. The asymmetric relation between interpreter and interpreted fuelled a lively public debate in the first part of the nineteenth century between 'restoring' or 'not restoring'. This is discussed through Eugène-Emmanuel Viollet-le-Duc's and John Ruskin's notions of authenticity as played out in relation to the invention that became key to the conceptualisation of heritage in the nineteenth century, that of photography.

This debate, between 'restoring' or 'not restoring', has also come to organise the narrative of conservation, structured around a dialectic between two diverging modes of practice; one that reconstructs in order to achieve a unity of style; the other, more antiquarian, that includes in the preservation all the changes and alterations that the building has suffered. In the history of conservation the contraposition of these two modes, identified by the figures of Viollet-le-Duc and Ruskin, has become an leitmotiv, repeated from Nicolaus Pevsner's influential essay "Scrape and Anti-scrape", 1976, to Jukka Jokilehto's crucial survey *A History of Architectural Conservation*, 1999, to OMA's CRONOCHAOS exhibition at the 2010 Architectural Biennale in Venice.[5] At one level this seems to describe the full horizon of strategies and actions in heritage and preservation. But on another level the debate can be understood not so much in terms of how you restore in one way or the other but as a fundamental question of authenticity related to forces of destruction. Restoration as it appeared in the nineteenth century threatened the integrity of the monument as a historical document on the one hand; on the other the absence of restoration threatened its very being as an historical object. Thus in these opposing and, in both cases, self-contradictory ideas about restoration the notion of a violation of the object of restoration is always at stake. The unity of style

Thomas Struth.
Stanze di Raffaello 2,
Rome 1990.
Chromogenic print.
Copyright Thomas Struth.

Thomas Struth.
National Gallery 1,
London 1989.
Chromogenic print.

approach usually requires interventions—the removal of accretions, the reconstruction of missing elements—all of which undermine the nature of the monument as an historical artefact that 'preserves' history. From an antiquarian position any kind of restoration is a threat. But to abandon the monument to the corrosive forces of nature and time would result in its degradation, and finally in its ceasing to be a monument.

At the turn of the twentieth century this conflict was identified and analysed in depth by the Austrian art-historian Alois Riegl in a text that has been central for this study, "The Modern Cult of Monuments; its Character and its Origin".[6] An examination of this text forms the basis of the third chapter. In his speculation on the monument Riegl put forward a thesis that takes the opposition between different modes of conservation as a base to suggest a fundamental redefinition of the monument from an object of weight, materiality and permanence to one of effect and disintegration.

Riegl emphasised that the tradition of erecting monuments for commemorative purposes was a diminishing, if not disappearing, activity in Western societies. The 'historical monument' on the other hand, he stressed, was increasing in its scope and reception. These 'historical monuments' were *ungewollte*, unintentional. Not purposely built as monuments they gained their value *a posteriori*; identified as irreplaceable links in the development of the Arts, they were venerated by an extending audience.[7] In Riegl's visually orientated analysis the gaze of the beholder was prioritised. The values he identified in the monument (commemorative-value, age-value and historical-value are examples) were classified according to the effect they generated upon the subject. Riegl's essay provides a unique perspective on the deep structures organising the desire for the past in a modern mass society and shows the fragility and transience that characterise the modern monument.

In the twentieth century the fragility of the monument has been mostly identified in relation to the forces of capitalism and urban modernisation, in which the architects of the Modern Movement have been the targets for extensive criticism. Accused of favouring their own artistic freedom before the values of the historic context, they became scapegoats in a rhetoric that tended to ignore the larger economic and political forces behind the reconfigurations of the European city. The origins of and contradictions in this account will be discussed through the emblematic case of Le Corbusier's radical urban proposal for Paris, the Plan Voisin, in chapter four. Despite the extensive destruction of the urban context proposed in the Voisin scheme, the position of the past here reveals Le Corbusier's debt to an antiquarian tradition of conservation emerging with the French Revolution. It also forms a pointer, or casts a shadow forward for a consideration of how ideas of heritage have been articulated in urban environments up until today. In particular, the possibility that the past can be 'zoned'—lifted physically, legislatively or in terms of identity away from the realm of the present—has had repercussions for the development of heritage policies during the later twentieth century. Similarly, Le Corbusier highlights the centrality of the visual in this new idea of the past, an assertion that appears indebted to both Riegl and Ruskin but which resonates forward in history towards the debates of the 1970s and 80s. Plan Voisin also countenances the shift from buildings to collections of buildings as the objects of conservation, and implies the extension of this expansion to landscapes and regions; both transfers have become central to conservation as played out globally in the international charters and conventions of organisations such as Unesco.[8]

Today the danger for heritage is changing its identity yet again. Aged, functionally inferior objects might appear logically superfluous to a western market economy that builds on the increasing consumption of products with shorter and shorter life-span. But what Robert Hewison in 1987 coined the "Heritage Industry" continues to grow and expand intensively.[9] In a society that loves the old, danger comes no longer from above but from below. With the extensive marketing of heritage and its overwhelming success in the popular realm, an increasing issue in the administration of the heritage site is how the heritage object can be protected not just from weather and neglect or the pressure of market-forces for commercial development, but from the wear and tear caused by the very lovers of the object: the heritage tourist. At the Unesco International Congress jubilee meeting of 2002, marking the thirtieth anniversary of the creation of the "World Heritage List", which took place in Venice—itself an object on the List—it was pointed out that the very object of the celebration had itself caused destruction. The classification into heritage risked the object's destruction rather than guaranteeing its protection.[10]

This increasing concern about fragility underlines the need to re-think the qualities that traditionally identify a monument, such as permanence or aesthetics. Rather it is the opposites of these qualities that monumentalise certain objects: qualities such as vulnerability, disintegration and destruction. Evidently this fragile monument is both generated by and therefore ultimately reliant on in the discourse of professions, international charters and organisations, and legal bodies for its existence.

THE HISTORIOGRAPHY OF CONSERVATION

Since the 1970s, when heritage entered a phase of critical re-assessment, a body of engaged critical literature has emerged in the field that in various ways tried to come to terms with its popularisation and commercialisation. The formidable success of heritage in the popular realm since the 1970s contrasts sharply with the often disappointed tone of these scholars, both when they defend heritage—Dan Cruickshank's *The Rape of Britain*, 1975; Patrick Cormack's *Heritage in Danger*, 1976; Wim Denslagen's *Architectural Restoration in Western Europe* and Jukka, Jokilehto's *A History of Architectural Conservation*, 1999—or when they attack its negative effects: David Lowenthal's *The Past is a Foreign Country*, 1985; Robert Hewison's *The Heritage*

Industry, 1987; Patrick Wright's *On Living in an Old Country: The National Past In Contemporary Britain*, 1985, and Françoise Choay's *L'allégorie du patrimoine*, 1992.[11]

The findings and reasoning in the present book draw strongly from this field, specifically Françoise Choay's ground-breaking analysis. This body of work however is rooted finally in a view of the history of conservation as a dialectic between two diverging modes of practice: conservation versus restoration. This dialectical model suggests a historical progress and synthesis in which the controversy of opinion between the different restoration strategies is resolved by a fuller and more complete understanding of authenticity. Yet this historiographical model, and the terminology belonging to it are underwritten by a value judgement that tends to repress the very unsettled nature of the authentic that is at the core of any conservation. Authenticity is identified no longer with any ideal historical form but with a building's actual materiality or its processual re-making. Rather than subscribing to this historiographical model, this present study suggests that some of the central perspectives underpinning the discourse and practice of conservation remain to be opened up in order to grasp the cult of the past today. Authenticity, origin and authorship are concepts at the core of the polemic that has surrounded conservation throughout its history. By studying that debate, the aim is to reveal the dominant and complex status these concepts still hold and how they have organised the discipline on both a conscious and an unconscious level.

This objective relates to my somewhat stubborn insistence that conservation is a modern phenomenon, generated out of the events that radically transformed western society around 1800. This proposition however is not put forward in order to identify a point of origin for conservation; evidently the 'care-taking' of buildings has, like architecture, no beginning. Rather the objective is to understand the cultural role of conservation at a specific moment in history; to ask at what moment did the maintenance and renewal of buildings shift to a discursive practice of conservation generating professions, schools and legal measures. Indeed how and when has the task of maintaining buildings become a site of conflicting and contradicting desires? This book provides if not a history, then a set of critical 'sites' that show how acts of saving, preserving and collecting objects have participated in constructing the notion of the historical monument, through relations based in power, instruction or sentiment.

NOTES

[1] Rossi, Aldo, *The Architecture of the City (L'architettura della città)*, Padua: Marsilio Editori, 1966), Diane Ghirardo and Joan Ockman trans., Cambridge MA., and London: MIT Press, 1989, p. 60.

[2] Nora, Pierre, "Between Memory and History", Marc Roudebush trans., *Representations*, 26, Spring, 1989, pp. 7–25.

[3] See Rücker, Frédéric, *Les Origines de la conservation des monuments historiques en France, 1790–1830*, Paris: Jouve & Cie, 1913, and further chapter 1: "The Space of Conservation".

[4] For passed acts and legislation on heritage in Europe in the nineteenth century see: Gerard Baldwin Brown, *The care of ancient monuments: an account of the legislative and other measures adopted in European Countries for protecting ancient monuments and objects and scenes of natural beauty, and for preserving the aspect of historical cities* (1905), reprinted Cambridge: Cambridge University Press, 2010.

[5] Pevsner, Nikolaus, "Scrape and anti-scrape", *The future of the Past. Attitudes to conservation 1174–1974*, Jane Fawcett ed., London: Thames & Hudson, 1976; Jokilehto, Jukka, *A History of Architectural Conservation*, Oxford: Butterworth-Heinemann, 1999; Office of Metropolitan Architecture, CRONOCHAOS, Exhibition, Venice Biennale, 2010.

[6] Riegl, Alois, "The Modern Cult of Monuments: Its Character and Its Origin" ("Der moderne Denkmalkultus. Sein Wesen und seine Entstehung", Vienna, 1903, republished in *Konservieren, nicht restaurieren. Streitschriften zur Denkmalpflege um 1900*, Bauwelt Fundamente, Braunschweig: Friedr. Vieweg & Sohn, 1988), Kurt Forster and Diane Ghirardo trans., in *Oppositions*, 25, 1982, pp. 21–51.

[7] Riegl, Alois, "The Modern Cult of Monuments: Its Character and Its Origin", Kurt Forster and Diane Ghirardo trans., in *Oppositions*, 25, 1982, pp. 21–51

[8] Unesco, United Nations Educational, Scientific and Cultural Organization. The proposal for a World Heritage Convention was launched at the Human Environment conference 1972 in Stockholm and later adopted at the General conference of Unesco in Paris the same year (16 November): Convention concerning the Protection of the World Cultural and Natural Heritage. See Unesco 1972, Convention Concerning the Protection of the World Cultural and Natural Heritage, Paris: Unesco, 1972. For the background history of the convention and the formation of Unesco's heritage engagement see: Lucia Allais *Will To War; Will To Art; Cultural Internationalism and the Modernist Aesthetics of Monuments*, Unpublished PhD

dissertation, MIT, 2008. Allais specifically emphasises the connection between war and the formation of international heritage. In an elegant analysis of the rescue of the Abu Simbel temples in Egypt she points to the role of heritage in cold war diplomacy. See also Turtinen, Jan, *Världsarvets villkor: Intressen, förhandlingar och bruk i internationell politik*, Stockholm: Acta Universitatis Stockholmiensis, 2006.

[9] Hewison, Robert, *The Heritage Industry: Britain in a Climate of Decline*, London: Methuen, 1987.

[10] The international Congress was organised by Unesco's World Heritage Centre and Regional Bureau for Science in Europe (ROSTE) with support of the Italian Government on the occasion of the 30th anniversary of the World Heritage Convention. The meeting took place in Venice. See further Paolo Costa presentation from the meeting summarised in the proceedings: *World Heritage 2002; Shared legacy, common responsiblity*, (Paris:World Heritage Centre, Unesco, 2003). See also Johansson, Andreas, "Turism och föroreningar hotar Italiens kulturarv", *Dagens Nyheter*, 21 November, 2002.

[11] Pevsner, Nikolaus, "Scrape and anti-scrape" in *The future of the Past. Attitudes to conservation 1174–1974*, Jane Fawcett ed., London: Thames & Hudson, 1976. Cruickshank, Dan, *The Rape of Britain*, London: Paul Elek, 1975; Cormack, Patrick, *Heritage in Danger*, London: New English Library, 1976; Denslagen, Wim, *Architectural Restoration in Western Europe: Controversy and Continuity*, Amsterdam: Architectura & Natura Press, 1994; Lowenthal, David, *The Past is a Foreign Country*, Cambridge: Cambridge University Press, 1985, Hewison, Robert, *The Heritage Industry: Britain in a Climate of Decline*, London: Methuen, 1987; Wright, Patrick, *On Living in an Old Country: The National Past In Contemporary Britain*, London: Verso, 1985; Choay, Françoise, *L'allégorie du patrimoine*, Paris: Seuil, 1992.

THE SPACE OF CONSERVATION

"Both the word and the thing are modern" Eugène-Emmanuel Viollet-le-Duc famously observes at the opening of his section on restoration in the *Dictionnaire raisonné de l'architecture française du XIe au XVIe siècle*, 1854–1868.[1] Viollet-le-Duc argued that his era, and his era alone, assumed a new analytic attitude to the past that implicated a new understanding of restoration. Many conservation historians have wanted to backdate Viollet-le-Duc's claim as to the radical novelty of restoration. In his influential essay "Scrape and anti-Scrape", Nikolaus Pevsner suggests that the library of St Johns College in Cambridge, built in 1624, reveals for the first time a sensitivity towards history, an awareness of the notion of anachronism that implies an understanding of style. Alois Riegl in his essay "The Modern Cult of Monuments; Its Character and Its Origin" makes a similar point, identifying the Renaissance rediscovery of Antiquity as the beginning of the modern notion of conservation.[2] These authors were neither the first nor the last to place the origin of a modern notion of conservation in the Renaissance period; indeed the Renaissance as a turning point for the history of conservation is generally acknowledged amongst restoration scholars.[3]

Rather than following Pevsner's and Riegl's thread, I will research the implications behind Viollet-le-Duc's claim. The background to the emergence of a modern discourse of conservation lay not, it will be argued, in an increasing appreciation of the monuments of Antiquity, slowly developing, step by step to an appreciation of all historical monuments (a model that implies that the appreciation of the past always starts from the 'top'). Instead, this chapter gives a more violent and disturbing beginning to the idea of caring for the past, by focussing on the emergent discourse of conservation that followed the French Revolution.

The destruction of art under the French Revolution has been a touchstone in the evaluation of the Revolution as whole. Radical historians have tended to play down the significance and effect of this iconoclasm. Conservative readings have placed Revolutionary vandalism at the beginning of a threatening genealogy of insurrection and anarchy contaminating the nineteenth century.[4] In that negative reading the

conservation of art is seen as the struggle of a few individuals against the overwhelming violence of the Terror.[5] This type of interpretation poses a simple opposition between the destruction of art and its conservation that tends to hide a common inheritance. A closer look at the iconoclastic crisis of the French Revolution shows that the narrative of the history of conservation as a fight against the 'vandalist' element of modernity has to be elaborated. The massive flow of decrees and laws concerning the protection of monuments during the Revolution shows intriguing interdependencies between the practice of conservation and that of destruction, ones that undermine any clear opposition between the two. I will suggest that our contemporary love for the old was shaped in many respects by the events that followed the critical moment of 1789. A new notion of conservation was triggered to a great extent out of the practical question of how the Revolution should deal with objects associated with the propaganda of the ancien régime. This chapter will trace how the idea of the public museum emerged both as a result and a logical continuation of Revolutionary vandalism. As a new institutional space the museum played a part in redefining the relationship between man and objects, and this shift in relationship helped to establish the idea of conserving and caring for objects despite, or even because of, their association with the political system of the overthrown regime. In emphasising the role of space in this shifted relationship between man and objects, I argue that during the Revolution conservation was part of the same iconoclastic culture as the destruction it seems to counteract.

THE DISCOURSE OF CONSERVATION

In November 1789 the National Assembly in Paris passed legislation to dispossess the church of its property.[6] Motivated by the same economic pressures that fuelled the Revolution itself, this act had an intriguing and unforeseen effect; it contributed to the emergence of a Revolutionary discourse of conservation. The dispossession led to the unprecedented challenge of how to control, justify and govern the redistribution of property now *à la disposition de la nation*. The directions for the management, sale, or conservation of former church property, the *biens nationaux*, were rapidly created. In decrees by the *Comité des affaires ecclésiastiques* and the *Comité d'aliénation des biens nationaux*, practical measures were prescribed for the organisation of this huge transfer of objects. The administration of the 83 new *départements* that had replaced the *gouvernements* and the *généralités* of royal government, were ordered to make inventories; to simply catalogue nationalised property, specifically statues, paintings, books and manuscripts. *Dépôts* of a temporary or permanent kind were planned in which to assemble the confiscated *biens*. To supervise this immense work a *Commission des monuments* was appointed in November 1790 with the task of formulating the methods and means for the classifications and the specifications that should direct the inventory.[7]

In this prescriptive work of the *Commission des monuments* a definition of national patrimony started to take form.[8] Although the idea of a collective heritage was not invented or originated with the Revolution, the confiscated *biens* generated a new need to clarify and specify the concept of patrimony. The very scale of the operation—firstly, the massive redistribution of objects belonging to the church; later the confiscation of property belonging to the monarchy and the *émigrés*—gave the notion of *patrimoine* an unprecedented importance.

The *dépôts* were central in the distillation of this new notion. As centres of re-distribution the *dépôts* became part of a process of purification and selection where the meaning of the objects they contained was held in suspense. The sheer mass of *biens* set in circulation through their uprooting from their normal context, their placement in the 'non-context' of the *dépôts* and museums, generated an interest in physical objects that went beyond their purely economic value.[9] These alienated objects in the *dépôts* gave rise to the idea of a physical form of national culture held in *trust* by the Nation for the public.[10] Indeed the emerging notion of heritage was closely linked to a 'duty of care' that in one sense challenged the original purpose of that nationalisation which was, one should not forget, brought forward by the Assembly to solve the acute financial crisis of 1789.

Through the liquidation of church property it was hoped to bring in ready money to run the country and, crucially, to handle the national dept, inherited from the *ancien régime*, that threatened to bankrupt France at the time. However, with the emerging discourse of conservation these *biens* ceased to be strictly commodities. A value was recognised in these former cult objects of the church that exceeded or replaced their exchange value and, through the various decrees and *ad hoc* legislation of preservation presented by the Revolutionary authorities, these confiscated objects were protected from sale on the open market. Classified as *patrimoine* these now very special objects were to be relocated into the realm of cultural history, a space that I will recognise here already generically, if not physically, as that of the museum. Indeed, as will become clear, it is from the French Revolution and onwards that the concept of heritage and museum cannot be thought of without one another.

MONUMENTS HISTORIQUES

The antiquarian Aubin Louis Millin's monumental project of making an illustrated 'catalogue' of France's newly nationalised "monuments", *Antiquités nationales ou Recueil de monumens* can illustrate this point.[11] The four volume publication, hastily published between 1790–1791, was driven by a threat of ruin very different from a financial one. As a supporter of the Revolution, Millin did not deny the economic possibilities gained by the confiscation of church property, but he also warned that the Nation inevitably stood to lose if the sale of these assets was realised without discrimination:

> Reuniting church property with national estates, and the prompt and easy sale of these estates will provide the nation with resources which, in its newfound freedom,

will make it the most happy and prosperous in the world: but we cannot deny that this hasty sale may strike a fatal blow to both the arts and the sciences, destroying works of genius and historical monuments whose preservation is of great concern.[12]

The introduction of the term "*monumen[t]s historiques*" is crucial in the re-evaluation of ecclesiastical objects and monuments.[13] Millin's plea for preservation, his opposition to sale, is justified by designating 'history' to the religious object; the value of the monuments resides no longer in their function as part of a Christian cult but in their historicity; detached from their original owner, the church, they gain a new function as a memory of the historical process that led to the triumph of the Revolution. Indeed, as I will emphasise when discussing the Revolutionary museum, the narration of the grand events of French history becomes dependent on the monument as witness to the success of history itself. Millin's notion of the *monument historique* is therefore central to the Revolution's construction of a national heritage in which the monument became an integrated part of a state controlled politics of memory.

Selection was at the core of this new notion of national heritage emerging out of Millin's concept of *monuments historiques*—for not all confiscated objects qualified as heritage. In the *Commission des monuments'* decree of 3 March, 1791, criteria were stated to define whether an object was worthy of conservation as an alternative to being sold or reused in other forms (i.e. melted down in the case of metal objects or used as mortar in the case of marbles). The object in question had either to be of historic interest, beautifully crafted, or to possess a pedagogic or technical value to the Arts.[14] The criteria for preservation listed presents a shift towards the establishment of a 'modern' notion of heritage that will distinguish Revolutionary discourses on conservation from earlier traditions of the restoration and maintenance of monuments.

In the *Instructions* the universalising idealism of the *Académie* is challenged and replaced by an all-inclusive notion of everything's value in the grand development of history. Noticeably, for example, the *Instructions* specially mention that Medieval monuments should be protected.[15] This new sensitivity would deprive Antiquity of any absolute value and lead to an idea of heritage where the relative value of every epoch was acknowledged. This in turn would effect the role of the past and its monuments; no longer would the ancient monument primarily function as an ideal model to be imitated, as it had in the discourse of architecture since the early Renaissance and the canonising texts of Alberti, but rather the notion of *monuments historiques* would turn the historical monument into a site of reflection in which the success or failure of the present epoch would be mirrored. It is in this sense one has to understand the cultural preservation of the French Revolution as part of a social renewal; the preservation of objects as 'historical' was indeed a way of breaking rather than connecting with the past.

After the suppression of the Academy, following the fall of the King, a new *Commission des arts* was appointed in September 1793 by the Jacobin Republic.[16] The confiscation of the property of the *Roi* and the *émigrés* expanded the types of objects that reached the *dépôts*; the task of the new commission was to supervise their management. The name of the committee was later changed to the *Commission temporaire des arts* and, after some conflicts, it replaced the original *Commission des monuments*.[17] The *Commission temporaire des arts* put forward new instructions for inventory and conservation, "*Instruction sur la manière d'inventorier et de conserver, dans toute l'étendue de la République, tous les objets qui peuvent servir aux arts, aux sciences et à l'enseignement...*" that, as the title suggests, expanded the scope of heritage beyond art and literature to all objects of service to the Arts and to education.[18] In line with the non-hierarchical taxonomy of the *Encyclopédie*, art, architecture, scientific objects as well as applied arts were all placed on the same level in the *Instruction*. This homogenisation of heritage was the inevitable result of Millin's concept of *monuments historiques* and anticipates the nineteenth and twentieth century expansion of conservation into all areas in society. Indeed the Revolution engendered an unprecedented debate on how to understand works of art, specifically architecture, as a form of historical evidence necessary to conserve for posterity; a debate in which the very concept of national heritage was crystallised.

DESTRUCTION AND CONSERVATION

This new sensibility to heritage, that can be read in both the Assembly's and the Jacobin Republic's legislation, contrasts with the iconoclasm that makes up the traditional imagery of the Revolution. Acts of destruction rather than conservation have dominated the historiography of the Revolution. Indeed, Revolutionary vandalism has remained, throughout the nineteenth and twentieth centuries, at the centre of a polemic between partisans and adversaries of the Revolution.[19] My objective here is, specifically, to avoid evaluating either the extent of Revolutionary vandalism or the success/failure of Revolutionary conservation. Rather the aim is to consider how the polemics of the debate itself have imprinted onto our minds an opposition between conservation and destruction that hides a common inheritance.

The horrifying narratives of the actions of violent mobs and calculating fanatics vandalising monuments tend to disguise the crucial role both iconoclasm and conservation had in the Revolutionary construction of "heritage". This is evident in Louis Réau's *Histoire du vandalisme*, 1959, were the Jacobin Republic is singled out as the sole agent of Revolutionary violence against art:

> They are determined to abolish the past, as if the past, which continues to live on in each of us, could be wiped out with the single stroke of a pen... In the sphere of the arts, the Revolution has been nothing but a devastating cyclone: it has sown no seeds for the future harvest of anything it has destroyed.[20]

Jacques Bertaux.
Destruction of the Equestrian Statue of Louis XIV, 1792.
Pen and ink drawing.
Museé du Louvre, Paris.
Copyright RMN-GP (Musée du Louvre/Michèle Bellot).

Réau's condemnation of Revolutionary conservation as hypocritical conforms to a dominant historiography in which Revolutionary vandalism appears as a scandal whose content is more commemorative than explicable. As Daniel Herman synthetically points out in his essay *Destructions et vandalisme pendant la Révolution Française*, the account of acts of vandalism falls within a logic of ideological denunciation that tends to reproduce, rather than unwrap, the polemic of the Revolutionary discourse on vandalism.[21]

A similar reduction appears when the new notion of conservation is attributed to the work of some few brave individuals heroically fighting against Revolutionary violence. This narrative was partly constructed by the self-appointed heroes themselves, figures such as Abbé Grégoire, dominant in the Revolution's debate on vandalism, and Alexander Lenoire, keeper of the *Musée des monumens français*. Grégoire describes in his *Mémoires* his fearful fight against vandalism, and Lenoire is not shy of heroising, in the *Description* that accompanies the collection of the *Musée des monumens français*, his achievement against all odds in saving architectural monuments from destruction.[22] The mythologies created by both figures about their specific roles in ending the overwhelming violence of the Revolution tend to be rehearsed by later scholars.[23] However neither type of condemnatory narrative takes into account the fact that legislation for the protection of monuments was in place from the early stages of the Revolution and, indeed, was developed further rather than abolished during the Terror associated with the Jacobin Republic.

The first part of this chapter has emphasised the Revolution's work of establishing a corpus of national heritage through the conservation of the monument. In observing this, one must acknowledge the use of destruction in the Revolutionary political programme. Put briefly, from the fall of the Bastille in 1789 throughout the period of the Jacobin Republic, iconoclasm played an important rhetorical role in every stage of the Revolutionary process, making change apparent and apparently irreversible. It was government policy after 1792 to eradicate signs of feudalism and superstition. On 14

August 1792, a decree ordered the *"suppression des monuments, restes de la féodalité"* and on 9 October 1793, *"tous les signes de royauté et féodalité"*.[24] Simultaneously, as has been noted, the *Commission temporaire des arts* worked out refined methods for classification and conservation in the *Instruction sur la manière d'inventorier* and presented decrees specifically forbidding the mutilation of objects which were of interest to art, history or to education.[25]

The issue here is to understand how within Revolutionary rhetoric the conservation of monuments was brought forward. One of the strongest and most enlightening contributions to the history of conservation in the field of architecture is Françoise Choay's *L'allégorie du patrimoine*, 1992.[26] For Choay conservation develops in two distinct phases during the Revolution. The first is defined as "preventative" (*préventive*) conservation, generated out of the immediate measures taken to safeguard newly nationalised works of art from violence. In part the threat is identified with the pillage, theft and general degradation which took place in the absence of law during the unstable periods of the Revolution. Within this category Choay also includes the destruction of monuments for their immediate military use; the removal and melting down for arms of the lead or copper roofs of cathedrals as well as the destruction of monuments for more direct economic reasons; the profitable use of monuments as quarries for building materials for example. Choay defines all these types of destruction as "non-political"; a form against which the efforts of "preventive" conservation are directed.

The second phase of conservation emerging out of the Revolutionary destruction that Choay identifies is "reactive" conservation (*réactionelle*), mainly appearing after the fall of the King in 1792. This *conservation réactionelle* differentiates itself from the *préventive* kind through its more methodical and refinedly argued procedures. Choay argues that these procedures are explicitly elaborated to fight against ideological destruction, the Revolution's iconoclasm as the state-sanctioned attack and destruction of monuments or any objects representing the hierarchy and power of the monarch, the nobility and the Church.[27] (One can note here that Choay, like Réau, grants no meaning to the violence of the mob, which is considered both irrational and "normal", while Jacobin iconoclasm carried out from the 'top' is political and extreme i.e. full of "meaning").

Although, as will become clear, it has limitations, Choay's distinction between different forms of destruction is useful, opening a more complex reading of Revolutionary conservation and destruction. The new concern for conservation is read as an urgent response to the cultural disaster of the Revolution, and the various commissions and decrees for the protection of art are elaborated specifically to fight the pillage and disfigurement of monuments. However to read the new notion of conservation as a direct counteraction to the cultural destruction associated with the Revolution leaves unresolved the question of the Revolutionary authorities' double engagement in conservation and destruction. As Choay herself points out, it is paradoxical that *conservation réactionelle* emanates, if not from the same committee members, from the same Revolutionary apparatus as the ideological iconoclasm which it appears to contradict; organised as an assistant commission to the *Comité d'instruction publique*, the *Commission temporaire des arts* was well integrated into the political organisation of the Revolutionary Government.[28]

This leads Choay to read the double objective of the conservation of works of art and the destruction of the symbols of the *ancien régime* as a paradoxical contradiction that reflects the complex state of political relations between the different committees.[29] In her analysis conservation and destruction are understood as each other's radical opposites; they are therefore not possible to maintain within the same political programme.

THE INVENTION OF VANDALISM

It would be overhasty, however, to accept this dichotomy at face value. It is possible to read the conflict Choay identifies between protective and destructive action within the cultural programme of the Revolution, less as a conflict between destroying and preserving objects than as a dispute over classification and appropriation.

The Revolutionary objective of purifying the past from the tyranny and prejudice associated with the old political system posed the delicate problem of how the Revolution, the protector of the Enlightenment, could support the Arts and at the same time condemn its former protagonist, the *ancien régime*. In a debate in the National convention, 1792, Jean Dusaulx made the problem clear in his references to the Port Saint-Denis in Paris:

> ... dedicated to Louis XIV, the proudest of all tyrants, it should be hated by all free men. But this portal is a masterpiece and, at small cost, could become a national monument.[30]

Dusaulx's aesthetic appropriation of Port Saint-Denis introduced a theme of dissociation between monument and symbol and further between the symbol and the institution it represented. This would become a dominant theme in the Revolution's inflamed debate on vandalism, where the argument would be used to condemn attacks on those cultural objects which were associated with a despised past.[31] Indeed the inability to separate between signifier and signified would itself, in anti-vandalistic discourse, become the definition of a vandal. This discourse created a certain politics of exclusion in which the appropriation and transformation of the monuments of the *ancien régime* was to become a prerogative of a rising cultural elite.[32]

Dominique Poulot makes a similar point in his profound analysis of the vandalistic debate during the Revolutionary years, a study that has been crucial for the argument in this chapter. In the essay "Revolutionary 'Vandalism' and the Birth of the Museum: The Effects of a Representation of Modern Cultural Terror" Poulot put forward intriguing arguments that suggest a revision of the binary interpretation of conservation versus destruction.[33] In contradistinction to Choay Poulot suggests that the Revolution's flow of decrees and *ad hoc* legislation concerning the protection of monuments must be understood not as a response to an overwhelming wave of iconoclasm but part of forming a new relationship to the past, a relationship in which heritage appears as the recognition of the past in the name of a general will and in accordance with criteria developed in the reign of criticism. Conservation and destruction are understood as different but closely interlinked means to come to terms with this new relation that was profoundly reliant on a revised understanding about the power of objects and their meaning.

In this interpretation the Revolution's acts both of violence and conservation are not understood as a series of means to achieve rationally calculated or evaluated ends. Rather the iconoclastic crisis of the Revolution reveals an extremely complex conflict of antagonistic classifications of objects whose traditional significance was regarded as suspended, a phenomenon that determined acts of conservation and destruction in order to redefine the meaning of the object. This in turn would assert an unprecedented civic responsibility towards past works of art that is still implemented in our contemporary protection and care for the past.[34] However in order to elaborate this new civic responsibility in relation to conservation it is necessary to rehearse the history of the word vandalism, a neologism that belongs to the Revolution.

The introduction of the term can be traced to Abbé Grégoire, constitutional bishop of Bois and a member of the Convention.[35] In 1794 Grégoire presented the first of his famous series of three reports written for the *Comité d'instruction publique: Rapport sur les destructions opérées par le Vandalisme, et sur les moyens de le réprimer.*[36] The reports express an urgent need to save treasures of art from the misguided and meaningless destruction of vandals. Not yet touched by the 'light' of knowledge, Grégoire's vandal destroyed in blindness and without discrimination. Logically this destruction could not be part of the cultural programme of the Revolution, that, after all, was the propagator of the Enlightenment. In Grégoire's words: "... barbarians and slaves hate the sciences and destroy artistic monuments: free men love them and seek to preserve them."[37]

The term vandalism was quickly assimilated into common parlance where, as Poulot has pointed out, it provided a focal point to a complex and even unintelligible event.[38] It was carefully chosen by Grégoire to describe the violation of monuments; in his memoirs he wrote "I created the word to kill the thing".[39] Even if there lay some exaggeration in Grégoire's claim of inventing the term, its association with the barbarian world of Goths and Vandals—with the Dark Ages—successfully repressed the fact that destruction was part of enlightened Revolutionary practice.[40] The reports, which were written by Grégoire partly as a defence from the accusation that the Comité itself, because of its Jacobean and Robespierrist origin, had been involved in the destruction of art, were effective in situating vandalism outside the discourse of the Revolution as something foreign to Revolutionary practice.[41] Even before Grégoire termed it 'vandalism' the destruction of art had been attributed by Revolutionaries to forces opposed to civilisation and the enlightenment project; in the very early stages of the Revolution such destruction was even attributed to counter-Revolutionary plots set up by members of the aristocracy in order to destroy the image of Revolutionary France.[42]

Grégoire's reports reinforced the image of the vandal as a threatening figure involved in counter-revolutionary conspiracies corrupting the Revolution's objectives:

> **But this new series of crimes should be associated with all other crimes by our enemies: to show that they wanted to destroy our political community through the wiping out of morals and learning.[43]**

This emphasis shifts in an intriguing way as the reports progress, with Grégoire accusing a section of the Revolutionary elite themselves of organising the destruction.[44] The notion of vandalism as something alien invading from outside was replaced with the perception of an interior threat: the Terror itself being identified with the negative forces destroying the Revolution.[45] In the aftermath of the denunciation of Robespierre and his cronies, the "9th Thermidor", this threat was primarily put down to Robespierre personally; for Grégoire, Robespierre the tyrant and Robespierre the vandal became one and the same.[46]

In the reports Grégoire drew up a list of scientific and artistic works that had been vandalised, a kind of negative catalogue mirroring the inventory list of the Commission des monuments. But as the itinerary and scope of vandalism grew from one report to another Grégoire mixed facts with rumours and fantasy revealing the difficulty of defining what constitutes an act as vandalistic.[47] Combining denunciation with an indictment of those responsible, Grégoire's reports, as Herman has highlighted, were mainly used to sift the guilty from the innocent, creating and developing a particular political culture of the Other.[48] One can note that Grégoire, along with the anti-vandalist discourse he inspired, established the link between terrorism and vandalism which has been a crucial element in the condemnation of vandalism ever since.

Pierre Etienne Le Sueur
*Vandal, destroyer of the
products of the Arts*,
1806, Gouache.
Musée Carnavalet, Paris.
Copyright Photothèque des
musées de la ville de Paris.

Indeed, as Poulot has insisted, Grégoire's anti-vandalistic discourse helped to establish the notion of a national heritage belonging to everyone by codifying the perception that any attack on monuments must be seen as an attack on society as a whole.[49] A new form of civic responsibility towards material culture was suggested that condemned any attack on the *objets nationaux* as a negative immoral form of expression: "Public respect is due above all to national objects, which belonging to nobody, are the property of everybody."[50]

Once the problem was understood to exist in a defect of character, a lack of knowledge which was properly barbarian, a trail began to be threaded back from individual acts of destruction to figures whose association with those acts revealed their inability to judge what objects were historically or artistically important. Ultimately this logic of denunciation led full circle to criticism of the *Commissions* themselves. Embedded in the whole system of classification of heritage that was developed by the *Commission des monuments* and the *Commission temporaire des arts* was the function of disqualification that in itself denied an object posterity and which therefore contributed, if in a passive way, towards its destruction. One of the greatest dangers to the monuments was therefore the threat of non-acknowledgement: a failure to be identified as valuable or significant was to be left outside the *catalogue*— and the discourse.

This theme of accusing the officials of neglect, of lack of ability to identify the unique value of an object in danger, would become a recurrent theme in discourses of conservation. Ruskin's condemnation of the restoration of Venice's palaces in the nineteenth century; the List of World Heritage in Danger from Unesco; contemporary activist groups united in order to save endangered species in architecture: all share with the French Revolution's discourse on vandalism a topos of threat that dominates the notion of heritage in Western culture.

THE SPACE OF CONSERVATION

A closer analysis of revolutionary vandalism shows that the relation between acts of destruction and their condemnation was vague and shifting.[51] The debate on vandalism contributed however to establishing a series of attitudes that still effect our relation towards the past. Indeed, as will be shown in the subsequent chapters, vandalist discourse contributed to forming a novel relation to the object that would make possible the dominant role that heritage came to assume in Western culture. In order to further question the binary interpretation of conservation-versus-destruction that the very discourse on vandalism helped to establish, it is crucial to reflect on the role of space in the iconoclasm of the Revolution.

From the beginning of the Revolution liberty was linked to the right to enter spaces that before had been the privilege of the few. One of the first delights of the Revolution was the beating down of gates, the crossing of castle moats, the rambling at ease in places once forbidden to enter.[52] This re-conquest of space was a way of symbolically breaking the continuity of the old order by traversing the spatial boundaries that previously had organised difference in society.

A famous but also intriguing example of such spatial appropriation was the demolishing of the Bastille, the old royal fortress and prison dominating the centre of Paris. At the time of the storming in 1789 its function as a prison was more or less redundant. But its heavy wall seems to have embodied a threat, on both a military and symbolic level, of a return of the old order.[53] Millin, in his *Antiquités nationales* described the energy surrounding the demolition of this symbol of royal despotism *par excellence*, whose destruction was later chosen to define the inauguration to the Revolution:

> Work was carried out with great speed, each day saw its proud towers grow ever smaller. Certain citizens kept stones, nails and other pieces of debris from the Bastille like precious monuments: one imagined them making inkwells from the stone or setting fragments into rings and selling these inkwells and this jewellery even in foreign countries.[54]

Millin's description is intriguing; the reuse of the Bastille's hated stones commemorated the fortress at the same time as a theme of miniaturisation—inkpots, rings—suggested a triumphal appropriation through the inversion of scale. This theme is even more exaggerated in the miniature replicas of the fortress laboriously carved out of the debris, examples of which are to be found in the collection of Musée Carnivalet in Paris today. These 'multiples' were distributed across France to the different departments as part of a conscious campaign to commemorate the event: "to perpetuate the horror of despotism".[55] This transformation of the fortress into many replicas made of and out of itself shows that on one level the Revolution

TOP Pierre-Antoine De Machy. *Destruction of the Bastille 17 July, 1789.* Oil on canvas. Musée Carnavalet, Paris. Copyright Photothèque des musées de la ville de Paris

BOTTOM P-F Palloy. Model of the Bastille made from a stone from the fortress. Musée Carnavalet, Paris. Copyright Photothèque des musées de la ville de Paris

was dependent on the very same symbols it despised. The double exercise of both destroying and, through an extreme form of reuse, conserving the Bastille turned it into an emblem of Revolutionary liberty as well as an indexical memento of the former oppression. (There is, as Dario Gamboni has pointed out, a ready analogue between the destiny of the Bastille and the modern example of the Berlin Wall. Like the Bastille the fragments of the Berlin wall quickly became collectable tokens commemorating the end of the Cold War. Not only were they widely spread geographically—they could be bought by postal order—but the larger pieces were used as political gifts and were

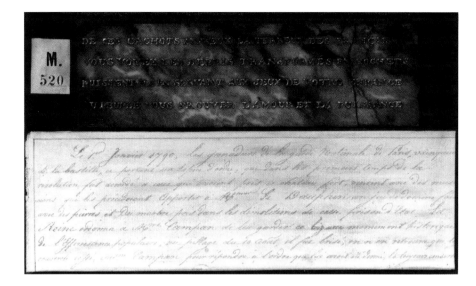

A lid for the box of a domino set made from the stones of Bastille, Museé Carnavalet, Paris.
Copyright Photothèque des musées de la ville de Paris.

installed among other places in the Vatican Gardens and near the Grand Arch de la Défense in Paris).[56]

After the Bastille had been demolished "right down to its foundations" even the site was commemorated in this double manner.[57] Under the supervision of the 'developer' Palloy, who had a monopoly on the production of mementoes from the Bastille, the site of the former fortress was converted into an open ballroom and trees were planted there. After innumerable projects had been submitted to commemorate the Revolution, any attempt to erect another building was abandoned and the place of the former fortress was kept as un-built. This sort of commemoration through absence must have been enhanced both by the function of the ballroom, suggesting movement rather than confinement, and by the greenery evoking images of the openness of the countryside rather than the enclosure of the former prison.[58]

Among the Revolution's acts of appropriation the example of the Bastille remains exceptional, but it offers the opportunity to revise the binary opposition between destruction and conservation that, through vandalist discourse, has affected the understanding of Revolutionary iconoclasm. I have argued that although destroyed, the Bastille was simultaneously conserved; through a radical transformation of its structure it continued to exist in the miniature replicas and the *bijoux*. However its spatial context was fundamentally and totally transformed, not just through its new minute and intimate scale but also in its new mobility and multiplicity that set up a different set of spatial relationships that 'destroyed' the former meaning of the monument at the same time as commemorating it.

The appropriation of the Bastille is reflected, if in a less extreme manner, in the Revolution's undertaking to transform the urban landscape in accordance with

its political programme. In its role of managing nationalised cultural property the Revolution conserved the monuments on the Nation's behalf; part of the Revolution's self-identity as a child of the enlightenment was it's cultural, and more specifically, educational vocation. However this educational vocation was carried out with the condition that any sights not worthy of the liberated citizen were eliminated or re-framed. Accompanied by an intriguing rhetoric of wounded gazes and intolerable sights the Revolution used spatial devices in order to in their view liberate the city from the legacy of the *ancien régime*.[59]

Underscored by an ideal of generating an urban space which was by definition democratic, a wide range of objects were seen to insult or threaten the liberated citizen purely through their presence in the urban landscape. Arms and effigies of the monarch, members of the nobility and the Church were systematically attacked but even more far reaching objects such as towers, because their verticality expressed hierarchy, or garden-follies, because of their association with luxury, could be deemed enemies of the Revolution. [60]

Crucially however, the Revolution's transformation of urban space was less about the total eradication of objects associated with the *ancien régime* than about changing their original meaning. Elimination was only one of the ways to disengage artefacts representing the old order. Other means of neutralising or transforming their meaning were the replacement or removal of visual signs and inscriptions; re-naming and re-dedication; the transformation or replacement of whole works; and the removal of monuments from their public site to other spaces, predominantly the museum.[61] In this urban reconfiguration the difference between acts of destruction and conservation is hard to define; rather, in the Revolution's regeneration of urban space, acts both of destruction and conservation were part of an iconoclastic culture conditioned by an exaggerated attention to the effect of images.

THE MUSEUM

This interdependence of destruction and conservation becomes evident in the Revolutionary museum.[62] A closer look at the organisation of the *Musée des monuments français*, established during the Revolution to exhibit architecture and sculpture, reveals how this double effect was achieved.

The history of the museum has always been closely linked to Alexandre Lenoir, an undistinguished painter who was the student of Pierre-Gabriel Doyen, a member of *commission des arts*. After the confiscation of church property in 1790, the *Comité d'aliéntation des biens nationaux* designated the convent of the Petits-Augustins as a *dépôt* for statues, marbles and bronzes (*matières métalliques*) of religious origin and, on the advice of Doyen, Lenoir was appointed as the *dépôt*'s overseer.[63] From the beginning of his new career Lenoir seems to have overstepped the role given to him as controller (*gardien*) and using his position, he started to search out objects; architectural monuments, sculpture and tombs were dismantled and brought to the *dépôt*.

This acquisition of objects, carried out under the direction of Lenoir, would distinguish the *dépôt* of the Petits-Augustins from the other *dépôts* that were simply storing objects awaiting their future designation. Through the conscious addition of objects Lenoir would turn the Petits-Augustins into a 'collection' of national monuments. When the primary symbol of the alliance between the Catholic Church and the throne, the church of Saint-Denis, was deconsecrated in 1793, Lenoir intervened and was able to have the sculptures of the royal tombs and other debris from the church transported to the Petits-Augustins.[64]

The collection of these royal monuments, over 400 of them, according to Lenoir, became the stimulus which transformed the *dépôt* into a museum.[65] During the festival in honour of the Constitution in the autumn of 1793, Lenoir was ordered to open up the collection to the public in order to let visitors from the different departments of France examine with their own eyes "des objets d'art que ce Dépôt renferme".[66] Two years later, in October 1795, the *Comité d'instruction publique* officially accepted Lenoir's programme for a

> **… a specialised museum, historical and chronological, where it will be possible to see the different periods of French sculpture in different rooms; each room bearing the character and exact physiognomy of the century it represents.**[67]

The former *dépôt* became the *Musée des monuments français*, a branch of the national museums under the authority of the Louvre, with Lenoir appointed as *conservateur*.[68] It is crucial to acknowledge here that the rescue of monuments from the destruction of 'vandalism', on which Lenoir prided himself, was not at odds with the Republican abolition of a despotic past. Indeed, as the various letters and directions from the *Commission du musée* and the Minister of Interior, Bénézech show, Lenoir enjoyed full support despite some organisational issues from the Revolutionary authorities in turning the *dépôt* of the Petits-Augustins into a public museum.[69]

That these two contradictory ambitions could be realised simultaneously—the abolition of a despotic past and the conservation of the objects that were understood as part of its rhetoric of power—relied principally on the mechanisms of spatial dislocation and representation which Lenoir's project involved. Until the closure of the museum in 1816 under the Bourbon government Lenoir was to elaborate and refine his strategies for exhibiting the dislocated objects.

From a first *salle d'introduction* where a range of sculptural objects from antiquity to the seventeenth century were displayed chronologically as a sort of pretext to the museum, the visitors moved on to the more specific historical rooms divided by century. In the overall chronological scheme these rooms were installed with appropriate fragments of monuments, and decorated to emphasise a sense of the century they represented. Lenoir brought this design principle to bear even on the illumination of the rooms. The first room, illustrating the thirteenth century, was decorated with the fragments Lenoir had collected from St Denis. Lit through coloured glass the room was dark and gloomy:

> **The shadowy illumination in this place even more evokes the time: the magic by which superstition struck such fear into a people that were in a perpetual state of weakness; I have noted that as we ascend the centuries growing closer to our own the light grows stronger in public monuments, as if the sight of the sun cannot be hidden from the educated man.[70]**

The overall rhetoric of the museum was synthesised in this lighting device.[71] The daylight virtually absent from this first room was increased successively as the progress of history was narrated from one room to another ending literally in the Age of Enlightenment. The spatial sequence of the museum projected 'a history' for the new era of the Revolution; a history of superstition and darkness that, through the Revolution, turned into one of enlightenment and happiness. The chronological order unfolding within the didactic space of the museum restored the 'vandalised' monuments to their proper place in history—at the very same instant that this chronology was the efficient device that destroyed the symbolic power of the monument. When placed in their original setting in Saint-Denis the royal tombs suggested that royal power and adoration were part of the Christian cult. The Revolutionary museum broke that link by conserving the same monuments as 'history'. Incorporated into a foreign discourse—the history of art—the monuments' original function of representing royal power was effectively replaced with a new function of instruction. As Lenoir formulated it in his programme for the museum:

In order to present a century so far removed from our own to enthusiasts of art and history, I tried to take into account all the most colourful and varied details....[72]

In this respect it is interesting that Lenoir's obsession of giving the right 'colour' to the historical rooms both emphasised the passage of time, by alienating the old from the present—the older the more obscure—at the same time as bringing these estranged centuries 'closer' through the metonymic process of representing a whole century by a few disparate and heterogeneous fragments. Later I will argue that this play between proximity and distance would become a prevailing theme in the dissemination of heritage to a larger audience.

Of all the spatial devices the Revolution employed to regenerate urban space the museum stands out as the most intriguing and innovative; indeed in the Petits-Augustins the iconoclastic crisis of the Revolution appears to have found its solution. The museum removed uncomfortable objects from their original site of conflict at the same time as it functioned as a storeroom that protected its contents from physical damage. Outside its original setting the force of the object, the possibility to harm or insult the viewer, vanished neutralised by the museum's didactic setting of art history. The Revolutionary museum appears then both an instrument and a result of iconoclasm engendered by a remarkable belief in the direct influence of space upon the public.

This belief in the power of space by the Revolutionaries was directly linked to the idea of utopia popularised through a century of writings by reformist, hygienist urbanists and architects.[73] In that thinking the issue of the past will always be complex and controversial. Indeed, the very belief in space as regenerative suggests that it must be emptied of other contradictory spaces telling different stories. The past as one such competitive narrative would have to be exiled from the homogenous space of utopia. This chapter has argued that the Revolutionary museum, as a new type of institution, can be understood as the first such space of exile for the past: in one gesture it both conserved and destroyed the symbols of the *ancien régime*. In that sense the Revolutionary museum fundamentally differed from the *Wunderkammer*, the Royal or private collection that has often been suggested as its predecessor.[74]

The Revolutionary museum reversed the homogenous space of utopia and in its confined space a less desirable past could be conserved; removed to another semantic field the antithetical associations of an object's symbolising power and hierarchy were transformed. Evicted from the re-generated spaces of the Revolutionary city, re-assembled and confined to the museum, the monuments of the *ancien régime* represented the tangible evidence of a new form of knowledge: the history of the Nation. It was in this sense that as a novel form of public space—the museum—the Petits-Augustins commemorated above all the finitude

Ici l'on Danse.

Vue de la Decoration et Illumination faite sur le Terrein de la Bastille pour le jour de la Fête de la Confédération Française le 14 Juillet 1790.

A Paris chez J. Chereau Rue St Jacques pres la Fontaine St Severin aux 2 Colonnes N.° 257.

Anonymous.
Dance and people's banquet given on the ruins of the Bastille, 14 July, 1790.

of the royal dynasty whose memories were appropriated and exhibited in a new spatial order.[75] But more crucially, with its double process of fragmentation and conservation the Revolutionary museum transformed the monument from an instrument of domination into one of instruction, a transformation, I would argue, that opened the way for a modern concept of heritage. Here, the monument is conserved and studied in order to gain knowledge (and in that sense morally improve the viewer) rather than to invoke fear and admiration.[76]

Jean–Lubin Vauzelle.
The introduction gallery,
Musée des Monuments
Français, Petits-Augustins,
1804, Oil on canvas.
Musée Carnavalet, Paris.

Léon Matthieu Cochereau
Gallery of the thirteenth
century, Musée des
Monuments Français,
Petits-Augustins, 1816,
Oil on canvas. Musée
Carnavalet, Paris.
Copyright Photothèque
des musées de la ville
de Paris.

Charles Marie Bouton
Sculpture gallery,
fortheenth century, Musée
des Monuments Français,
Petits-Augustins,
Oil on canvas. Musée
Carnavalet, Paris.
Copyright Photothèque des
musées de la ville de Paris.

Gallery of the fifteenth
century, Musée des
Monuments Français,
Petits-Augustins.
Oil on canvas. Musée
Carnavalet, Paris.
Copyright Photothèque des
musées de la ville de Paris.

CONSERVATION OR DESTRUCTION OF ART

While today the museum is largely associated with the protection of objects, at the time of its formation as a state institution in France the complex alliance between preservation and destruction carried out within its walls was acknowledged and discussed. Was the museum a place that conserved or destroyed art? This dispute was thrown into relief by the debate that was to accompany Napoleon's project to establish the ultimate museum in the wake of the Revolutionary wars of Europe. The plan to assemble "trophies of conquest", art treasures confiscated in the various campaigns, would create a museum that turned Paris into the centre of the art world and provide concrete and glorious evidence of Napoleonic victories.

Most outspoken and clear in his critique against the Revolutionary museum was the artist and art historian Antoine Chrysotôme Quatremère de Quincy, who occupied for a few decades the centre of official cultural discourse in France. Both a man of the Revolution closely associated with the leaders of early Revolutionary events and its adversary—he participated in counter-revolutionary activities—Quatremère was highly critical of Napoleon's imperialistic project.[77] When in hiding after being sentenced to death in 1796 he published "*Lettres à Miranda sur le déplacement des Monuments de l'art de l'Italie*", which drew attention to cultural effects of dislocating and transplanting artworks from their original settings. Quatremère argued that artworks could only be understood in the contexts in which they had been produced; to place them in the *conservatories* was the same as "killing art".[78]

Quatremère's claims were contradicted by, among others, François de Neufchâteau, once Minister for the Interior, and an outspoken supporter of Napoleon's seizure of art. While Quatremère saw the collection of objects in the museum as an act of alienation, Neufchâteau saw the transfer of art from Italy, Belgium and Holland to the free nation of France as an act of salvation. Bringing them on to republican soil would liberate and protect the artworks, giving them a resting-place in a free state where they could be made public and admired by free citizens. The repatriation of art and its display in the museum was a way to reward the sublime achievement of the dead artist, whose work had been locked up in, and perverted by the ignorance of, private religious collections.[79]

The salvation and dissemination of art through the institution of the museum, versus the critique of the museum's alienating effect, is a recurring conflict in the discourse of conservation. Neufchâteau's argument for the democratisation of art through acts of nationalisation has largely been implemented in the Western world. Quatremère's letters, on the other hand, started a theme of criticism that would follow the notion of conservation throughout its history and development, a critique underscored by a longing for authenticity and totality that will be explored in the following chapters.

I have emphasised in this chapter how the French Revolution's redistribution of property helped to generate a new type of object, the *monument historique*. This 'historisation' had a double edge however; folded into the realm of history the monument was qualified for preservation at the very same time that its new identity as an historical object revealed its inherent fragility. As 'history' it now existed in a form of afterlife, as an anachronism, always to be threatened by the very same notion of history that generated its value. The need for the museum as a new space in which this double game of ruination and conservation could find its logic of execution is evident in the Revolutionary discourse on conservation. From the French Revolution and onwards the concept of heritage and museum are implied in each other.

The museum, however, depended on a certain 'mobility' of objects that excluded a large part of the historical heritage, specifically architectural monuments. Returning to Millin's *Antiquités nationales*, 1790–1791 discussed at the start of this chapter one can see that it was specifically these limitations that motivated his grand project of documenting all of France's architectural monuments. In the prospectus Millin explains:

> For some time now we have been treating as a serious matter the reunion of Libraries and Paintings, but there is a vast amount of interesting artistic and historical objects which cannot be moved and which will doubtless be destroyed or vandalised. These are precious monuments that we have the intention of protecting from the destructive scythe of time.[80]

Left outside the museums and *dépôts* these 'immobile objects' identified by Millin remained unprotected, and exposed to the destructive force of time their ruination was inevitable. This ruination would generate a loss that undermined the creation of a national history: the catalogue of objects that together constituted that history would be incomplete, denying the full knowledge that, in the tradition of comparative history, could only be reached through a complete set.

It was to overcome this lack that Millin set out to execute detailed representations of the monuments of France: "Nothing shall be neglected in the attempt to render a faithful representation of the objects and their precise description."[81]

Choay has suggested that Millin's objective to conserve the monument through drawing reveals how he was still left in an Antiquarian tradition of abstract "iconographic conservation", a tradition, Choay argues, that with the French Revolution's wholesale acts of confiscation was to be challenged and replaced, almost overnight, with the actual conservation of physical objects.[82] However, I should suggest that Millin's desire to document the monuments so faithfully before they ceased to exist acutely reverses the antiquarian tradition of recovering lost monuments through an intellectual reconstruction on paper. In Millin's case the monument is still present but already thought of as a ruin; although not yet destroyed, it is already missed, evoking a desire to capture it before it is gone. Indeed the notion of the monument's tragic destiny has already turned it into an image of itself: "These are precious monuments which we have the intention of protecting from the destructive scythe of time."

I understand Millin's representation of the monuments as a form of proto-photography where the desire to arrest the passage of time through a process of automatic imprinting is felt already, although the technology is still lacking. This is revealed not least in Millin's reassuring promise to his future readers: "Nothing shall be neglected in the attempt to render a faithful representation of the objects." Linked to this desire to imprint rather than depict is the objective of redeeming the monuments from their anchored condition in the ground that, as ruins, they were predestined to return to. Reproduced as prints and assembled in four volumes the monuments gained a certain 'placelessness' that curiously offered them the very historical permanence that their monumental and permanent quality denied them.

In the next chapter I will reflect further on this desire to arrest the passage of time through automatic imprinting. I will look at how the new media of photography affected the restoration theories of John Ruskin and Eugène-Emmanuel Viollet-Le-Duc, specifically in relation to the concept of authenticity. Millin's term *"monument historique"* was strongly underwritten by a notion of authenticity inherited by nineteenth century historical discourse. Both Ruskin and Viollet-le-Duc turned to photography in search of authenticity. However, the photographic working of the image would make complicated the very notion of the authentic. The photographic imprint would awake a nostalgic desire to reinstate what will tentatively be defined as a "pre-modern" relation to the object. A relation that would be unmediated and spaceless, lacking the distance that is necessary for 'history' to take place.

BIBLIOGRAPHICAL SUMMARY

The French Revolution is one of the most written about events in Western history, and the approaches to its history are many sided and ideologically diverse. The historiography of the French Revolution is in itself a topic for research that goes well beyond the scope of this chapter. This chapter was previously published as "Bevarandets rum", *Agora: journal for metafysisk spekulasjon*, Oslo, 2006 and I have chosen to republish it here as it was written originally. The argument and the research for this chapter was undertaken mainly towards the end of the 1990s and the following literature was valuable for establishing the argument: *Histories: French Constructions of the Past* (*Histories: French Constructions of the Past, Post-war French Thought*, Jacques Revel and Lynn Hunt eds., New York: The New Press, Vol 1, 1995) has been useful for grasping the diversity in French historical thought. For a more specific understanding of the historiographical issues around the French Revolution the introduction to Lynn Hunt's *Politics, Culture and Class in the French Revolution*, Berkeley: University of California Press, 1984, has been useful as has François Furet's *Interpreting the French Revolution*, Cambridge: Cambridge University Press, (1981), 1988.

For the general history of the French Revolution this chapter has benefited from the following scholars work: Cobban, Alfred, *A History of Modern France, 1715–1799*, London: Penguin/Harmondsworth, 1983; Furet, François, *Revolutionary France 1770–1880*, Oxford: Blackwell, 1992; Furet, François and Ozouf, Mona, *A Critical Dictionary of the French Revolution*, Cambridge, MA: Harvard University Press, 1989; Sutherland, Donald, *France 1789–1815, Revolution and Counterrevolution*, London: Fontana Press, 1985.

For the history of vandalism Dario Gamboni's book *The Destruction of Art* was a productive entry into the topic, specifically its linking of the vandalism of the French Revolution to the more recent vandalism that took place after the fall of Soviet Union (Gamboni, Dario, *The Destruction of Art, Iconoclasm and Vandalism since the French Revolution*, London: Reaktion Books, 1997). David Freeberg's two books *Iconoclasts and their Motives* and *The Power of Images: Studies in the History and Theory of Response* as well as the various authors' essays in the collection *Vandalism: Behaviour and Motivations*, were all productive for developing the argument in the chapter (Freedberg, David, *Iconoclasts and their Motives*, Maarsen: G Schwartz, 1985; *The Power of Images: Studies in the History and Theory of Response*, Chicago and London: University of Chicago Press, 1989; Lévy-Leboyer, Claude, ed., *Vandalism: Behaviour and Motivations*, Amsterdam: North Holland, 1984).

For Revolutionary 'Vandalism' specifically, the argument put forward in this chapter was influenced by Dominique Poulot's essay "Revolutionary 'Vandalism' and the Birth of the Museum" (Poulot, Dominique, "Revolutionary 'Vandalism' and the Birth of the Museum: The Effects of a Representation of Modern Cultural Terror", *Art in Museums*, Susan Pearce ed., London: Athlone Press, 1995). Important was also Richard Wrigley's argument in the essay "Breaking the Code: Interpreting French Revolutionary Iconoclasm" (*Reflections on Revolution, Images of Romanticism*, Alison Yarrington and Kelvin Everest eds., London: Routledge, 1993). Other works helpful for developing the analysis have been: Eugène Despois, *Le vandalisme révolutionnaire*, Paris: Germer Baillière, 1848; Daniel Herman, "Destructions et vandalisme pendant la Révolution Française", *Annales ESC* 33, 1978; Stanley J Idzerda, "Iconoclasm During the French Revolution", *American Historical Review*, 60:1, 1954, pp. 13–26, and Pierre Marot, "L'abbé Grégoire et le vandalisme révolutionaire", *Revue de l'Art*, 49, 1980. pp. 36–39.

Mona Ozouf's remarkable study *Festivals and the French Revolution* contributed to formulate the argument on space and has also had a general methodological impact (Ozouf, Mona, *Festivals and the French Revolution*, Cambridge, MA, and London: Harvard University Press, 1988). For the history of Revolutionary conservation Françoise Choay's chapter on the French Revolution in her *L'allégorie du patrimoine* was crucial (Choay, Françoise, *L'allégorie du patrimoine*, Paris: Seuil, 1992). Dominique Poulot's, *Musée, nation, patrimoine: 1789–1815* complemented Choay's work in its discursive analysis of the role of conservation and national heritage in Revolutionary France (Poulot, Dominique, *Musée, nation, patrimoine: 1789–1815*, Paris: Éditions Gallimard, 1997). For the history of the various committees' engagement in conservation during the Revolution, Frédéric Rücker's *Les Origines de la conservation des monuments historiques en France, 1790–1830* was very useful (Rücker, Frédéric, *Les Origines de la conservation des monuments historiques en France, 1790–1830*, Paris: Jouve & Cie, 1913).

For the history of the revolutionary museum Anthony Vidler's chapter "Architecture in the Museum" in *The Writings of the Wall* was an inspiring introduction to the Musée des Monuments Français (Vidler, Anthony, *The Writings of the Wall, Architectural Theory in the Late Enlightenment*, New York: Princeton Architectural Press, 1987). Dominique Poulot's contribution to Pierre Nora's *Les Lieux de Mémoire* helped to widen the perspective given by Vidler (Poulot, Dominique, "Alexandre Lenoir et les musées des monuments français" *Les Lieux de Mémoire*, II, Pierre Nora ed., Paris: Éditions Gallimard, 1992, pp. 497–526). Other useful literature was Louis Courajod, *Alexandre Lenoire et le Musée des Monuments Français*, Paris: Libraire Honoré Champion, 1878–1886, and Christopher Greene, "Alexandre Lenoire and the Musée des Monuments Français during the French Revolution" in *French Historical Studies*, Vol XII, No 2, Fall 1981, pp. 200–222.

PRIMARY SOURCES

Grégoire, Abbé Henri:

Instruction publique—Rapport sur les destructions opérées par le vandalisme et sur les moyens de le réprimer, Paris, 1794, pp. 1–28.

Second rapport sur le vandalisme, Paris, 1794, pp. 1–12.

Troisième rapport sur le vandalisme, Paris, 1795, pp. 1–21. Source: British Library, Bibliothèque Historique de la Révolution, BL: 772.3.4.

Mémoires, ed., H Carnot, Ambroise Dupont, Paris, 1837.

Millin, Aubin Louis:

Antiquités nationales ou Recueil de monumens pour servir à l'histoire générale et particulière de l'Empire française, 4 Vols., Paris, 1790–1795.

Prospectus presenting *Antiquités nationales ou Recueil de monumens*, Paris, 1790, p. 1. Source: British Library, French Tracts on Science, BL: 936.f.9 (28).

Lenoire, Alexandre:

Description historique et chronologique des monumens et des sculptures réunis au Musée des monumens français, septième édition, Paris, 1803.

NOTES

[1] Viollet-le-Duc, Eugène-Emmanuel, *On Restoration*, Sampson B Bucknall trans., London: Low, Marston, Low, and Searle, 1875, p. 1. From chapter "Restauration", in *Viollet-le-Duc, Eugène-Emmanuel, Dictionnaire raisonné de l'architecture française du XIe au XVIe siècle*, Paris: B Bance, A Morel, Vol. 8, 1866.

[2] Pevsner, Nikolaus, "Scrape and anti-scrape", *The future of the Past. Attitudes to conservation 1174–1974*, Jane Fawcett ed., 1976, and Riegl, Alois, "The Modern Cult of Monuments: Its Character and Its Origin", (*Der moderne Denkmalkultus. Sein Wesen und seine Entstehung*), Vienna, 1903 republished in *Konservieren, nicht restaurieren. Streitschriften zur Denkmalpflege um 1900*, Braunschweig: Bauwelt Fundamente, Friedr. Vieweg & Sohn, 1988), Kurt Forster and Diane Ghirardo trans., *Oppositions*, 25, 1982, pp. 21–51.

[3] See for example: Denslagen, Wim, *Architectural Restoration in Western Europe: Controversy and Continuity*, Amsterdam: Architectura & Natura Press, 1994; Choay, Françoise, *Paris: L'allégorie du patrimoine*, 1992; Jokilehto, Jukka, *A History of Architectural Conservation*, Oxford: Butterworth-Heinemann, 1999.

[4] See Herman, Daniel, "Destructions et vandalisme pendant la Révolution Française", *Annales ESC*, 33, 1978, pp. 703–705.

[5] See for example Georges Lefebvre's description of Alexandre Lenoire's fight against "vandalisme" in Lefebvre, Georges, *La France sous le Directoire, 1795–1799*, Paris: Éditions Sociales, 1977, pp. 577–578, and further Réau, Louis, *Histoire du vandalisme. Les monuments détruits de l'art française*, 1958, augmented edition Michel Fleury and Guy-Michel Leproux eds., Paris: Robert Laffont, 1994, p. 513; Marot, Pierre "L'abbé Grégoire et la vandalisme révolutionaire", *Revue de l'Art*, 49, 1980, pp. 36–39; Vidler, Anthony, *The Writings of the Wall: Architectural Theory in the Late Enlightenment*, New York: Princeton Architectural Press, 1987, p. 169.

[6] For a summary of the economic background to the confiscation of church property see Doyle, William, *The Oxford History of the French Revolution*, Oxford: Clarendon Press, 1989, pp. 134–135. See also Rücker, Frédéric, *Les Origines de la conservation des monuments historiques en France, 1790–1830*, Paris: Jouve & Cie, 1913, p. 13. For a general history of the French Revolution see François Furet, *Revolutionary France 1770–1880*, Oxford: Blackwell, 1992.

[7] Frédéric Rücker in his thesis *Les origines de la conservation des monuments historiques en France, 1913*, has assembled and analysed the different decrees and legislation that followed the dispossession, Rücker,

Frédéric, *Les Origines de la conservation des monuments historiques en France, 1790–1830*, Paris: Jouve & Cie, 1913, p. 53–78. See also further the *Procès-verbaux du Comité d'instruction publique de l'Assemblée Législative, Collection des Documents Inédits sur l'histoire de France*, published and annotated with a commentary by MJ Guillaume, Paris: Librairie Hachette et Cie, 1889, pp. i–xxiv.

[8] Rücker, Frédéric, *Les Origines de la conservation des monuments historiques en France, 1790–1830*, Paris: Jouve & Cie, 1913, pp. 64–67.

[9] See Dominique Poulot's argument about the dépôts as part of a "rite d'instauration" in Poulot, Dominique, *Musée, nation, patrimoine: 1789–1815*, Paris: Éditions Gallimard, 1997, pp. 136–139. See also Choay, Françoise, *L'allégorie du patrimoine*, Paris: Seuil, 1992, pp. 78–79.

[10] A point emphasised by Dominique Poulot (Poulot, Dominique, *Musée, nation, patrimoine: 1789–1815*, pp. 189–191). See also, by the same author, "Revolutionary 'Vandalism' and the Birth of the Museum: The Effects of a Representation of Modern Cultural Terror", in *Art in Museums*, Susan Pearce ed., Athlone Press, London, 1995, p. 203.

[11] Millin, Aubin Louis, *Antiquités nationales ou Recueil de monumens pour servir à l'histoire générale et particulière de l'Empire française*, Paris: 6 vols., 1790–1795, (the first four volumes published 1790–1792). Millin, Aubin Louis (1759–1818) was an antiquarian and naturalist. A founding member of *Société Linnéenne*, in 1794 he was appointed as *Conservateur du Cabinet des médailles*.

[12] "La réunion des biens écclésiastiques aux domaines nationaux, la vente prompte et facile des ces domaines, vont procurer à la nation des ressources, qui, sous l'influence de la liberté, la rendront la plus heureuse et la plus florissante de l'univers: mais on ne peut disconvenir que cette vent précipitée ne soit, pour le moment, très-funeste aux arts et aux sciences, en détruisant des productions du génie et des monumens historiques qu'il serait intéressant de conserver." The quote by Millin is taken from the prospectus presenting *Antiquités nationales ou Recueil de monumens*, Paris, 1790, p. 1. Souce: British Library, French Tracts on Science, BL: 936.f.9 (28.)

[13] The modern spelling of "monuments" will be used henceforth in referring to this concept.

[14] Rücker, Frédéric, *Les origines de la conservation des monuments historiques en France, 1790–1830*, Paris: Jouve & Cie, 1913, pp. 66–67; see also Choay, Françoise, *L'allégorie du patrimoine*, Paris: Seuil, 1992, pp. 84.

[15] Rücker, Frédéric, *Les origines de la conservation des monuments historiques en France, 1790–1830*, pp. 66–67.

[16] Rücker, Frédéric, *Les origines de la conservation des monuments historiques en France, 1790–1830*, pp. 78–80.

[17] For the history of the conflict between the Commission des monuments and Commission temporaire des arts see "Introduction" to Louis M Tuetey, *Procès-verbaux de la commission temporaire des arts*, Paris: Librairie Ernest Leroux, 1912, pp. i–xxxix. See also Pierre Marot, "L'abbé Grégoire et le vandalisme révolutionaire", *Revue de l'Art*, 49, 1980, pp. 36–39.

[18] Rücker, Frédéric, *Les origines de la conservation des monuments historiques en France, 1790–1830*, Paris: Jouve & Cie, 1913, p. 94.

[19] See Herman, Daniel, "Destructions et vandalisme pendant la Révolution Française", *Annales ESC*, 33, 1978, pp. 703–705.

[20] "Leur idée fixe est abolition du passé, comme si le passé, toujours vivant en chacun de nous, pouvait être effacé d'un trait de plume. Dans le domaine de l'art, la Révolution n'a été qu'un cyclone dévastateur: elle n'a rien semé, à la place de ce qu'elle avait détruit, pour préparer les futures moissons" from Réau, Louis, *Histoire du vandalisme. Les monuments détruits de l'art française*, 1958, augmented edition Michel Fleury and Guy-Michel Leproux eds., Paris: Robert Laffont, 1994, p. 542.

[21] Herman, Daniel, "Destructions et vandalisme pendant la Révolution Française", *Annales ESC*, 33, 1978, p. 705.

[22] Lenoire, Alexandre, *Description historique et chronologique des monumens et des sculptures rénuis au Musée des monumens français*, septième édition, Paris, 1803, p. 2; and *Grégoire, Abbé Henri-Baptiste, Mémoires*, Paris: H Carnot ed., 1837, Vol. II, pp. 345–352.

[23] Denslagen, Wim, *Architectural Restoration in Western Europe: Controversy and Continuity*, Amsterdam: Architectura & Natura Press, 1994; Jokilehto, Jukka, *A History of Architectural Conservation*, Oxford: Butterworth-Heinemann, 1999; Greene, Christopher, "Alexandre Lenoire and the Musée des Monuments Français during the French Revolution", in *French Historical Studies*, Vol. XII No. 2, Fall 1981, pp. 200–222.

[24] Quoted in Rücker, Frédéric, *Les origines de la conservation des monuments historiques en France, 1790–1830*, Paris: Jouve & Cie, 1913, pp. 21–25. On

the dominant role of violence in the imagery of the Revolution see further Gamboni, Dario, *The Destruction of Art*, London: Reaktion Books, 1997, pp. 31–36.

25 Rücker, Frédéric, *Les origines de la conservation des monuments historiques en France, 1790–1830*, pp. 13–21.

26 Choay, Françoise, *L'allégorie du patrimoine*, Paris: Seuil, 1992.

27 Choay, Françoise, *L'allégorie du patrimoine*, pp. 83–86.

28 For the history of the *Commission temporaire des arts* see "Introduction" in Tuetey, Louis M, *Procès-Verbaux de la commission temporaire des arts*, Paris: Librairie Ernest Leroux, 1912, pp. v–xxxix.

29 Choay, Françoise, *L'allégorie du patrimoine*, Paris: Seuil, 1992, p. 87.

30 "... consacrée à Louis XIV, au plus fier des despotes, elle mérite toute la haine des hommes libres. Mais cette porte est un chef-d'oeuvre, et à peu de frais elle peut être convertie en un monument national." Quoted in Edouard Pommier, "Discourse iconoclaste, discourse culturel, discourse national. 1790–1794", in *Révolution Française et "Vandalisme" Révolutionaire*, Paris: Universitas, 1992, p. 311.

31 See further Poulot, Dominique, "Revolutionary 'Vandalism' and the Birth of the Museum: The Effects of a Representation of Modern Cultural Terror", in *Art in Museums*, Susan Pearce ed., London: Athlone Press, 1995, pp. 192–213; see also Gamboni, Dario, *The Destruction of Art*, London: Reaktion Books, 1997, pp. 35–36.

32 Herman, Daniel, "Destructions et vandalisme pendant la Révolution Française", *Annales ESC*, 33, 1978, pp. 703–705.

33 Poulot, Dominique, "Revolutionary 'Vandalism' and the Birth of the Museum: The Effects of a Representation of Modern Cultural Terror", in *Art in Museums*, Susan Pearce ed., London: Athlone Press, 1995, pp. 192–214, and, by the same author, chapter VI "L'angoisse des temps", in *Musée, nation, patrimoine: 1789–1815*, Paris: Éditions Gallimard, 1997, pp. 177–194.

34 Poulot, Dominique, "Revolutionary 'Vandalism' and the Birth of the Museum: The Effects of a Representation of Modern Cultural Terror", *Art in Museums*, Susan Pearce ed., London: Athlone Press, 1995, p. 208.

35 Grégoire, Henri-Baptiste, 1750–1831. A Cleric and politician, Grégoire was an early advocate of Jewish emancipation and throughout his life was also strongly engaged in the emancipation and enfranchisement of

the black population in the French Caribbean colonies. This together with his ideas about the formation of a national culture and a constitutional church was to define his political engagement. By 1789 he emerged as a spokesman for the lower clergy and favoured the reform of the church proposed by the Revolutionary government. He was one of five priests to take the Tennis Court Oath and he was a president of the National Assembly. After the fall of the King he was elected to the National Convention. Essentially sympathetic to Robespierre he was elected a member of the Committee of Public Instruction (*Comité d'instruction publique*) where he, among other things, worked for the organisation of national libraries and, as discussed in this chapter, for the preservation of works of art as national heritage. After 1795 Grégoire was elected to the Council of Five Hundred and 1801, despite his religious views and republicanism, he became a senator under Napoleon. With the Bourbon restoration, his political life ended and he retired to spend his final years in scholarship, writing mainly on church history and his memoirs.

36 *Grégoire, Abbé Henri, Instruction publique—Rapport sur les destructions opérées par le vandalisme et sur les moyens de le réprimer*, Paris, 1794. Source: BL: 772.3.4.

37 "Les barbares et les esclaves détestent les sciences, et détruisent les monuments des arts; les hommes libres les aiment et les conservent." Grégoire, Abbé Henri, *Instruction publique—Rapport sur les destructions opérées par le vandalisme et sur les moyens de le réprimer*, Paris, 1794. Source: BL: 772.3.4., p. 27.

38 Poulot, Dominique, "Revolutionary 'Vandalism' and the Birth of the Museum: The Effects of a Representation of Modern Cultural Terror", in *Art in Museums*, Susan Pearce ed., London: Athlone Press, 1995, p. 196.

39 *"Je créais le mot pour tuer la chose."* From *Gregoire's Mémoires*, H Carnot ed., Paris: Ambroise Dupont, 1837, Vol. 1, p. 346.

40 See Baczko, Bronislaw, "Vandalism", *A Critical Dictionary of the French Revolution*, François Furet and Mona Ozouf eds., Cambridge, MA: Harvard University Press, 1989, pp. 860–868.

41 Baczko, Bronislaw, "Vandalism", *A Critical Dictionary of the French Revolution*, pp. 860–868.

42 Tuetey, Louis M, *Procès-verbaux de la commission temporaire des arts*, Vol. 1, Paris: Librairie Ernest Leroux, 1912, p. 115.

43 "Mais il fallait joindre cette nouvelle série de crimes à tous les crimes de nos ennemis: Prouver qu'ils ont voulu dissoudre notre société politique par l'extinction de la morale et lumières." Grégoire, Abbé Henri, *Instruction publique—Rapport sur les destructions opérées par le vandalisme et sur les moyens de le réprimer*, Paris, 1794. Source: British Library, Bibliothèque Historique de la Révolution, BL: 772.3.4., p. 17.

44 Grégoire, Abbé Henri, *Instruction publique—Rapport sur les destructions opérées par le vandalisme et sur les moyens de le réprimer*, Paris, 1794. Source: British Library, Bibliothèque Historique de la Révolution, BL: 772.3.4., pp. 12–15.

45 Grégoire, Abbé Henri, *Instruction publique—Rapport sur les destructions opérées par le vandalisme et sur les moyens de le réprimer*, Paris, 1794. Source: British Library, Bibliothèque Historique de la Révolution, BL: 772.3.4., p. 13–15.

46 Baczko, Bronislaw, "Vandalism", in *A Critical Dictionary of the French Revolution*, François Furet and Mona Ozouf eds., Cambridge, MA: Harvard University Press, 1989, p. 861.

47 The reports on vandalism by Abbé Henri Grégoire are –*Instruction publique, Rapport sur les destructions opérées par le vandalisme et sur les moyens de le réprimer*, Paris, 1794, pp. 1–28. –*Second rapport sur le vandalisme*, Paris, 1794, pp. 1–12. –*Troisième rapport sur le vandalisme*, Paris, 1795, pp. 1–21. Source: British Library, Bibliothèque Historique de la Révolution, BL: 772.3.4. See specifically report number three where Grégoire lists vandalised objects region by region.

48 Daniel Herman has suggested that the Revolution's vandalistic debate was above all a form of political exclusion aimed at denying the popular classes access to the political realm. See Herman, Daniel, "Destructions et vandalisme pendant la Révolution Française", *Annales ESC*, 33, 1978, pp. 716. See also Poulot, Dominique, "Revolutionary 'Vandalism' and the Birth of the Museum: The Effects of a Representation of Modern Cultural Terror", in *Art in Museums*, Susan Pearce ed., London: Athlone Press 1995, p. 197.

49 Poulot, Dominique, "Revolutionary 'Vandalism' and the Birth of the Museum: The Effects of a Representation of Modern Cultural Terror", in *Art in Museums*, Susan Pearce ed., London: Athlone Press 1995, p. 203–204. See also Baczko, Bronislaw, "Vandalism", in *A Critical Dictionary of the French Revolution*, François Furet and Mona Ozouf eds., Cambridge, MA: Harvard University Press, 1989, p. 861.

50 "Que le respect public entoure particulièrement les objets nationaux, qui, n'étant à personne, sont la propriété de tous." Grégoire, Abbé Henri, *Instruction publique—Rapport sur les destructions opérées par le vandalisme et sur les

moyens de le réprimer*, Paris, 1794, p. 26. Dominique Poulot has emphasised this effect of the vandalistic discourse: Poulot, Dominique, "Revolutionary 'Vandalism' and the Birth of the Museum: The Effects of a Representation of Modern Cultural Terror", *Art in Museums*, Susan Pearce ed., London: Athlone Press, 1995, pp. 209–210.

51 Daniel Herman has underlined how the vandalistic debate mainly reflected political relations and ultimately class struggle. Dominique Poulot goes one step beyond this interest-orientated definition to suggest that revolutionary vandalism was to a large extent an effect of discourse rather than a response to any real threat to the heritage of France. See Herman, Daniel, "Destructions et vandalisme pendant la Révolution Française", *Annales ESC*, 33, 1978, pp. 703–719. Poulot, Dominique, *Musée, nation, patrimoine: 1789–1815*, Paris: Éditions Gallimard, 1997. See also by the same author "Revolutionary 'Vandalism' and the Birth of the Museum: The Effects of a Representation of Modern Cultural Terror, *Art in Museums*", Susan Pearce ed., London: Athlone Press 1995, pp. 192–214.

52 Ozouf, Mona, *Festivals and the French Revolution*, Cambridge, MA and London: Harvard University Press, 1988, pp. 126–157.

53 Réau, Louis, *Histoire du vandalisme. Les monuments détruits de l'art française*, 1958 augmented edition Michel Fleury and Guy-Michel Leproux eds., Paris: Robert Laffont, 1994, pp. 265–272.

54 "Les travaux furent poussés avec une grande activité, chaque jour on voyait diminuer l'orqueil de ses tours. Quelques citoyens conservèrent des pierres, des clous, et d'autres débris de la Bastille, comme des monumens précieux; on imagina de faire avec les pierre des encriers, on en incrusta même quelques parcelles dans des bagues, et on vendit de ces encriers et de ces bijoux jusques dans les pays étrangers...." Millin, Aubin Louis, *Antiquités nationales ou Recueil de monumens pour servir à l'histoire générale et particulière de l'Empire français*, 4 Vols., Paris, 1790–1795, Vol. 1, p. 15.

55 "... pour y perpétuer l'horreur du despotisme...." Quote from "Patriote Palloy" in Réau, Louis, *Histoire du vandalisme. Les monuments détruits de l'art française*, 1958 augmented edition Michel Fleury and Guy-Michel Leproux eds., Paris: Robert Laffont, 1994, p. 270.

56 Gamboni, Dario, *The Destruction of Art: Iconoclasm and Vandalism since the French Revolution*, London: Reaktion Books, 1997, pp. 60–62.

57 "... jusque dans ses fondements...." Quote from Patriote Palloy in Réau, Louis, *Histoire du vandalisme. Les monuments détruits de l'art française*, 1958, augmented edition Michel Fleury and Guy-Michel Leproux eds., Paris: Robert Laffont, 1994, p. 270.

58 See Simon Schama's vivid description of the afterlife of the Bastille in Schama, Simon, *Citizens, a Chronicle of the French Revolution*, New York: Alfred A Knopz, 1989, pp. 406–419, and the analytical description of Ozouf, Mona, *Festivals and the French Revolution*, Mass. and London: Harvard University Press, 1988, p. 149. See also Etlin, Richard A, *Symbolic Space: French Enlightenment Architecture and Its Legacy*, Chicago and London: University of Chicago Press, 1994, pp. 38–39.

59 See the rhetoric of the offended eye in Edouard Pommier's essay "La théorie des arts", *Aux armes et aux arts, Les arts de la Révolution 1789–1799*, Philippes Bordes and Régis Michel eds, Paris: Éditions Adam Biro, 1988, pp. 178–183.

60 Pommier, Edouard "La théorie des arts", *Aux armes et aux arts, Les arts de la Révolution 1789–1799*, pp. 178–183 and Poulot, Dominique, *Musée, nation, patrimoine: 1789–1815*, Paris: Éditions Gallimard, 1997, pp. 160–161.

61 A point made clear by Richard Wrigley in his intriguing essay "Breaking the Code: interpreting French Revolutionary iconoclasm" that has influenced my argument. Dario Gamboni in his crucial book *The Destruction of Art: Iconoclasm and Vandalism since the French Revolution* has underlined Wrigley's point, noting that elimination was only one of the ways to disengage artefacts representing the old order. Wrigley Richard, "Breaking the Code: Interpreting French Revolutionary Iconoclasm", *Reflections on Revolution, Images of Romanticism*, Alison Yarrington and Kelvin Everest eds., London: Routledge, 1993, pp. 182–194; Gamboni, Dario, *The Destruction of Art: Iconoclasm and Vandalism since the French Revolution*, London: Reaktion Books, 1997, pp. 31–36.

62 See further Stanley J Idzerda's synthetical argument in his article "Iconoclasm during the French Revolution", Idzerda, Stanley, J, "Iconoclasm during the French Revolution", *American Historical Review*, 60:1, 1954, pp. 13–26.

63 For the history and description of the museum see Courajod, Louis, *Alexandre Lenoire, son journal et le Musée des monuments français*, Paris: Libraire Honoré Champion, 1878–1886. For a critical discussion and comment on the role of the Musée des monuments français see Poulot, Dominique, "Alexandre Lenoir et les musées des monuments français" in *Les Lieux de Mémoire, La Nation*, Vol. 2, Pierre Nora ed., Paris: Édition Gallimard, 1992, pp. 497–526. See also Greene, Christopher, "Alexandre Lenoire and the Musée des Monuments Français during the French Revolution" in *French Historical Studies*, Vol. XII, No. 2, Fall 1981, pp.

200–222; and Vidler, Anthony, *The Writings of the Wall, Architectural Theory in the Late Enlightenment*, New York: Princeton Architectural Press, 1987, pp. 167–173.

64 Lenoire, Alexandre, *Description historique et chronologique des monumens et des sculptures renuis au Musée des monumens français*, septième édition, (catalogue for *Musée des monumens français*), Paris, 1803, p. 3. See also Louis Réau's description of Lenoir's activities in Réau, Louis, *Histoire du vandalisme. Les monuments détruits de l'art française*, 1958, augmented edition Michel Fleury and Guy-Michel Leproux eds., Paris: Robert Laffont, 1994, p. 397.

65 Lenoire, Alexandre, *Description historique et chronologique des monumens et des sculptures renuis au Musée des monumens français*, septième édition, (catalogue for Musée des monumens français), Paris, 1803, p. 3.

66 In a letter from *Le ministre de l'intérieur*, addressed to Lenoire and dated 3rd August 1793. Tuetey, Alexandre and Guiffrey, Jean, *La Commission du musée et la création du musée du Louvre*, Paris: Daupeley-Gouverneur, 1910, p. 244.

67 "Musée particulier, historique et chronologique, où l'on retrouvera les âges de la sculpture française dans des salles particulières, en donnant à chacune de ces salles le caractère, la physionomie exacte du siècle qu'elle doit représenter...." Lenoire, Alexandre, *Description historique et chronologique des monumens et des sculptures rénuis au Museé des monumens français*, septième édition, (catalogue for Musée des monumens français), Paris, 1803, p. 3.

68 Courajod, Louis, *Alexandre Lenoire, son journal et le Musée des monuments français*, Paris: Libraire Honoré Champion, 1878–1886, Vol. I, pp. clxii–clxiii.

69 Courajod, Louis, *Alexandre Lenoire, son journal et le Musée des monuments français*, Vol. I, pp. clxii–clxiv.

70 "La lumière sombre qui éclaire ce lieu est encore une imitation du temps; magie par laquelle on maintenait perpétuellement dans un état de faiblesse des êtres que la superstition avait frappés d'effroi; car j'ai observé que plus on remonte vers les siècles qui se rapprochent du nôtre, plus la lumière s'agrandit dans les monumens publics, comme si la vue du soleil ne pouvait convenir qu'à l'homme instruit." Lenoire, Alexandre, *Description historique et chronologique des monumens et des sculptures rénuis au Musée des monumens français*, septième édition, (catalogue for Musée des monumens français), Paris, 1803, p. 112.

71 Anthony Vidler has emphasised this in his analysis of the museum, see Vidler, Anthony, *The Writings of the*

Wall: Architectural Theory in the Late Enlightenment, New York: Princeton Architectural Press, 1987, pp. 170–172.

72 "Pour présenter aux amateurs des arts et de leur histoire la vue d'un siècle aussi éloigné, j'ai cherché à me rendre compte de tous ces détails qui peignent avec les couleurs les plus variées." Lenoire, Alexandre, Description historique et chronologique des monumens et des sculptures rénuis au Musée des monumens français, septième édition, (catalogue for Musée des monumens français), Paris, 1803, pp. 112–13.

73 For the symbolism of space and the belief in its regenerative force in the period of French Enlightenment see Etlin, Richard A, Symbolic Space: French Enlightment Architecture and Its Legacy, Chicago and London: University of Chicago Press, 1994. For a discussion of the role of space in different theories of institutional form in the period of the Enlightenment see: Vidler, Anthony, The Writings of the Wall: Architectural Theory in the Late Enlightenment, New York: Princeton Architectural Press, 1987, and Ozouf, Mona, Festivals and the French Revolution, Cambridge, MA and London: Harvard University Press, 1988, esp. Chapter VI, "The Festival and Space".

74 See further Tony Bennet's discussion of the Royal Art Gallery as precursor of the modern public art museum in the historiography of the museum, and the problems relating to this, (Bennett, Tony, The Birth of the Museum: History, Theory, Politics, London: Routledge, 1995, pp. 33–40). For the history of the exhibition strategies of the Cabinet of Curiosities, see Impey, Oliver and Arthur MacGregor, The Origins of the Museum: The Cabinet of Curiosities in Sixteenth- and Seventeenth-Century Europe, Oxford: Clarendon Press, 1985.

75 A point made by Poulot, see Poulot, Dominique, "Alexandre Lenoir et les musées des monuments français" in Les Lieux de Mémoire, La Nation, Vol. 2, Pierre Nora ed., Paris: Édition Gallimard, 1992, p. 513.

76 Dario Gamboni discusses Klaus Herding's analysis of vandalism in these terms. See Gamboni, Dario, The Destruction of Art, Iconoclasm and Vandalism since the French Revolution, London: Reaktion Books, 1997, pp. 36; and Herding, Klaus, "Denkmalsturz und Denkmalkult—Revolution und Ancien Regime", Nue Zürcher Zeitung, 30–31 January 1993.

77 For a thorough presentation of Quatremère de Quincy's theories of architecture see, Lavin, Sylvia, Quatremère de Quincy and the Invention of a Modern Language of Architecture, Cambridge, MA: MIT Press, 1992. For Quatremère's criticism of Napoleon's museum project see, Déotte, Jean-Louis "Rome, the Archetypal Museum and the Louvre, the Negation of Division" in Art

in Museums, Susan Pearce ed., London: Athlone Press 1995, pp. 215–232. See also the introductory essay in Lettres à Miranda sur les déplacements des monuments de l'art de Italie par Quatremère de Quincy, Edouard Pommier ed., Éditions Macula, Paris, 1989. For a study of the tension between Rome and Paris and how that took its expression in the restoration of monuments in Rome under Napoleon's reign, see, Jonsson, Marita, Monumentvårdens begynnelse: Restaureringar och Friläggning av antika monument i Rom 1800–1830, Stockholm: Uppsala Studies in the History of Art, Almquist & Wiksell International, 1976, pp. 45–105.

78 Quatremère de Quincy, Antoine Chrysotôme, "Lettres à Miranda sur le déplacement des Monuments de l'art de l'Italie" in Considérations morales sur la destination des ouvrages de l'art, (Rome, 1815), Paris: repr. Fayard, 1989, p. 48.

79 For a description of François de Neufchâteau's support of Napoleon's repatriation see, Déotte, Jean-Louis "Rome, the Archetypal Museum and the Louvre, the Negation of Division" in Art in Museums, Susan Pearce ed., London: Athlone Press, 1995, pp. 215–232.

80 "On s'est occupé depuis quelque temps plus sérieusement de la réunion des Bibliothèques et des Tableaux, mais il y a une foule d'objets intéressants pour les arts et pour l'histoire, qui ne peuvent être transportés, et qui seront infailliblement bientôt détruits ou dénaturés. Ce sont ces monuments précieux que nous avons formé le dessein d'enlever à la faux destructive du temps." The quote by Aubin Louis Millin is taken from the prospectus presenting Antiquités nationales ou Recueil de monumens, Paris, 1790, pp. 1–2. Source: British Library, French Tracts on Science, BL: 936.f.9 (28).

81 "Rien ne sera négligé pour la représentation fidèle des objets et pour la l'exactitude des descriptions." The quote by Aubin Louis Millin is taken from the prospectus presenting Antiquités nationales ou Recueil de monumens, Paris, 1790, pp. 1–2. Source: British Library, French Tracts on Science, BL: 936.f.9 (28). p. 4.

82 Choay, Françoise, L'allégorie du patrimoine, Paris: Seuil, 1992, p. 77.

THE
AUTHENTIC

OPPOSITE Eugène-Emmanuel Viollet-le-Duc. Exploded perspective of an arch. Published in *Dictionnaire raisonné de l'architecture française du XIe au XVIe siècle*, 1854–1868.

Restoration is conditioned by an underlying uncertainty about where its object is; whether to be found in an 'ideal' historical form, or in the actual physical appearance of the object that is to be restored. The search for the 'real' object in conservation is surrounded by this ambiguity; to distinguish between true and false, beginning and end, original and appliqué.

In the first part of the nineteenth century this ambiguous nature of the conservation object was at the centre of a lively public debate. The appearance of AW Pugin's *Contrast* in 1841 helped to create a common ground for discussion between the profession and the public; John Ruskin's *Seven Lamps of Architecture*, 1849, and *Stones of Venice*, 1851–1853, significantly broadened this base in England, while in France Victor Hugo's best-selling novel *Notre-Dame*, 1831, which features the historical cathedral as its main character, had a similar effect.[1] The impassioned arguments these authors presented, and which such a wide audience absorbed, were fired by a controversy about whether to "restore or not restore": restoration threatened the authenticity of the monument on the one hand; on the other, the absence of restoration threatened its very being.

This interest in issues of restoration, widely felt within a general European cultural discourse in the first part of the nineteenth century, coincided with the emergence of the discipline of photography. Indeed, the medium of photography was deeply implicated in the restoration debate. In 1851 the *Commission des monuments historiques* established a *Mission héliographique*, for which five photographers travelled France in order to document examples of endangered architectural heritage.[2] In England the Architectural Photographic Association was founded in 1857 with the ambition of forming a large collection of architectural photographs, mainly of historical monuments.[3]

This use of photography was to change fundamentally the way a wider audience was able to experience buildings. Through photographic imprints, distant buildings were suddenly brought closer, providing a visual knowledge of architecture that had

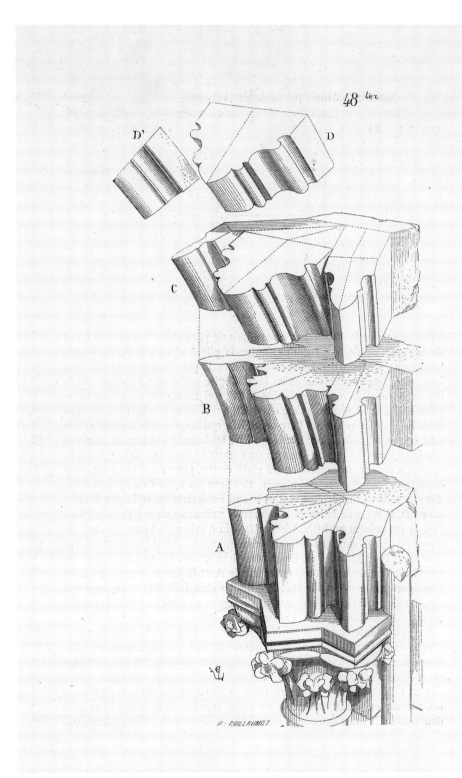

previously been the reserve of the travelled art connoisseur. But photography was also readily used in the process of restoration itself. Eugène-Emmanuel Viollet-le-Duc early underlined the potential of photographic documentation: "Photography, which assumes every day a more important phase in scientific studies seems to have appeared for the very purpose of aiding this grand work of restoration"; and John Ruskin, who used daguerreotypes to record buildings in Venice, wrote in a letter to his father in 1845: "It is certainly the most marvellous invention in the century; given us, I think, just in time to save some evidence from the great public of wreckers."[4]

Viollet-le-Duc's and Ruskin's contradictory ideas are a *leitmotif* in the literature on restoration.[5] It has been suggested that the two figures' attitudes can be related to different schools of restoration, or even that their different approaches result from opposing national characters, a point argued in Pevsner's essay on Englishness and Frenchness in the appreciation of the Gothic.[6] Ruskin has been called in to represent a more antiquarian approach to the monument, one in which all its history is to be included in its preservation, while Viollet-le-Duc has stood for the rational school that suggests reconstruction in order to achieve a unity of style.

Without denying the radical difference between Ruskin's and Viollet-le-Duc's theories of restoration, this chapter aims to bring forward aspects that are easily overlooked in such simplified divisions. By focussing on the notions of space and vision, an alternative framework in which to compare their ideas will be explored. Using their comments on photography as points of reference I will focus specifically on the effect the new media of photography exerted on the notion of the authentic for these two central figures in the history of conservation. The close links that so rapidly developed between restoration and photography in the early nineteenth century were not expedient or coincidental. Rather, these ties gained potency because the two disciplines were driven by a similar desire, inspired by and invested in concepts of time and nature that were undergoing a profound crisis of identity at this time.

NATIONAL HISTORY

In the previous chapter I argued that the event of the French revolution gave rise to a discourse of conservation that transformed the monument from an instrument of domination into an object of knowledge. This notion suggested that the history of the Nation had been recorded in the stones and joinery of buildings over the centuries and that this so far unarticulated knowledge could be spelled out. The mapping and organisation of this new national history unleashed a massive flow of drawing and writing on historical architecture of an unprecedented scale and scope.[7]

Writing in mid-nineteenth century France, Viollet-le-Duc was deeply engaged in this enterprise of constructing a national history in text and drawing. His literary pursuits are impressive; the *Dictionnaire raisonné de l'architecture française du Xie au XVIe siècle*, 1854–1868, his study of Gothic architecture, standing out as a nearly manic one-man enterprise that evolved from a project of just two volumes into a vast undertaking of ten volumes with a total of 5,000 pages and 3,367 images that took nearly 15 years to complete.[8] The *Dictionnaire*'s unprecedented way of linking text and drawing intimately together was to have a profound effect on the use of architectural drawing in historical writing.[9] The illustrations in the *Dictionnaire* convey with incredible virtuosity the materiality and spatiality of Gothic architecture; in analytical sections and exploded perspectives the assembly of the construction is exposed and analysed in detail. In his analysis of the *Dictionnaire* Barry Bergdoll has pointed out that these unprecedented kinds of drawing work in support of Viollet-le-Duc's polemic against Quatremère de Quincy and the *Academie*, that runs as a subtext throughout the *Dictionnaire*.[10] Quatremère de Quincy's theory of architecture as an essentially imitating art was undermined by Viollet-le-Duc's argument that the truth of the evolution of architecture was to be found at a deeper level, beyond the compositional and formal:

> Our age has adopted an attitude towards the past in which it stands quite alone among historical ages. It has undertaken to analyse the past, to compare and classify its phenomena, and to construct its veritable history, by following step by step the march, the progress, the successive phases of humanity....[11]

For Viollet-le-Duc the true origin of architecture was to be revealed through a methodical analysis of its construction. Every building had a history that could be re-told in a narrative of functionality where each part played a crucial role in constituting the whole.[12] In Viollet-le-Duc's notion of architectural building history nothing was superfluous or arbitrary, every part had a given function and place.[13] It was this re-writing of the history of architecture in terms of the functionality of form that made Viollet-le-Duc stand out as a progressive architect for the following generation; his emphasis on the rationality of historical form found resonance in the architectural theories of Frank Lloyd Wright and Le Corbusier among others.[14]

This rational study of historical construction that Viollet-le-Duc eagerly promoted had a larger scope, however. It would tell a corresponding narrative at a second level. The joining of building materials would not just give the answer to how ancient buildings were constructed but essential clues to the whole political and social structure of the society in which the building had originally been erected. In this archaeo/anthropological approach architecture was granted a primary role; indeed, for Viollet-le-Duc it became the main character in the history of the Nation.

RESTORATION

Viollet-le-Duc's involvement in the formation of a national history was not limited to writing and drawing; from a young age he was managing large restoration projects, noticeably the church in Vézelay and later, together with JBA Lassus, the important restoration of Notre-Dame in Paris. As a protégé of Prosper Mérimée, an influential intellectual in Parisian circles and director of the *Commission des monuments historiques*, Viollet-le-Duc was linked closely with the development of the *Commission*. The *Commission*, established in 1837 by the historian and politician François Guizot, systematically surveyed national patrimony and ranked it for protection and restoration.[15]

Photography would play a crucial role in this inventory. The *Mission héliographique* initiated by the *Commission* in 1851 employed photographers to travel France documenting endangered monuments in the provinces.[16] In the same year Viollet-le-Duc presented to the *Comité de la langue, de l'histoire et des arts de la France* photographs taken by Henri le Secq, one of the photographers from the *Mission héliographique*. The photographic images pictured sculptures, architectural details and ornamentation from the cathedrals of Paris, Reims, Amiens and Chartres. The demonstration led to the recommendation by the committee that all the important monuments of the Middle Ages be photographed.[17]

The photographic documentation reinforced the idea of the national monument, a notion that was born, as has been argued in the previous chapter, out of the cultural iconoclasm of the French Revolution. Like the various Revolutionary commissions the *Commission des monuments historiques*, as a new bureaucratic body organised from Paris, strove to gain control over the destiny of historic buildings in the provinces and a photographic record was part of such an effort. Indeed, the tension between Paris and the provinces that marked the vandalist debate of the Revolution (in Grégoire's argument the vandalism was always taking place in remote, obscure places) is likewise present in the grand restoration projects of nineteenth century France. The restorations, state sponsored and carried out under the supervision of the *Commission des monuments historiques*, challenged local control over historic buildings. As part of a network of historical sites the significance of the monument shifted from commemorating the local society into commemorating France at large.[18] What I want to underline here, and what was also argued in the previous chapter, is that the very definition of buildings as *historical monuments* would necessarily generate this shift from local to national. As will become evident, photography was part of such a process of redefinition on several levels.

THE NEED FOR HISTORY

In the introduction to the *Dictionnaire*, Viollet-le-Duc motivates his studies into Medieval architecture with the necessity for history; in order to advance man needs to take advantage of all the collected efforts of previous centuries: "in order to pave a path to the future, we need to know where we're from".[19] The study of history was a "need of the moment" too profound to be explained as a reaction to the destruction of the previous century. Indeed, for Viollet-le-Duc, when the love for the past contained reactionary ingredients triggered by the vandalism of the Revolution, the risk was that it turned into a fanaticism discouraging a serious approach to historical studies.[20] As Viollet-le-Duc underlines in several places in the *Dictionnaire* the study of the past was therefore not an attempt to reinstate the past; on the contrary a rational research into the past was the very means to leave that past and embrace the future:

> … the European has reached this phase in the development of the human intellect, that while advancing with redoubled speed towards the destinies of the future, and perhaps even because he advances thus rapidly, he feels the necessity of collecting all that belongs to his past—just as we collect a large library to prepare for future labours….[21]

The collection of this archive was facilitated by a new tool that in its very speed suggested that it could follow man's increasingly rapid advance into the future: the camera. In the introduction to the *Dictionnaire*, Viollet-le-Duc emphasises the crucial role of the new technological medium in documenting architecture. The camera, invented in the age of progress, was a medium that looked backward:

> It appears that new inventions are coming to the aid of this general tendency. At a moment when it seems the artist's hand is no longer adequate to record the very many precious remains of our ancient monuments, photography appears and compiles, in the space of a few years, a faithful inventory of the debris.[22]

When Viollet-le-Duc wrote this in 1854 he had already utilised this new medium of mechanical reproduction himself. He commissioned daguerreotypes to be taken of Notre-Dame as early as 1842, three years after Daguerre had presented his invention in Paris.[23] It is likely that the daguerreotypes were to be used in his and JBA Lassus' proposal for the restoration of Notre-Dame in Paris, presented to a restoration committee appointed in January 1843. Viollet-le-Duc and JBA Lassus won the commission and the extensive restoration work was begun in 1845 to be finished nearly two decades later in 1864. When completed previous alterations by royalty and clergy had been removed together with most traces of former repairs and restorations. Sculptures vandalised during the French Revolution were completed with new re-constructions and signs of any decay that the cathedral had suffered during six centuries were erased.[24]

The restoration of Notre-Dame was a prestigious commission and its development was followed both in France and abroad.[25] At the point at which Viollet-le-Duc's and Lassus' proposals for Notre-Dame were presented, a critical discussion and valuation of restoration was beginning to be voiced in the new and expanding architectural press. Viollet-le-Duc had already experienced the force of public criticism during his restoration of the church at Vézelay, and the reconfiguration of that church to represent a stage in the development of Gothic architecture had proved controversial to local opinion and clergy alike. He and Lassus took care to present the restoration of Notre-Dame, therefore, as a project both respectful to the monument and compatible with the requirements of religious practice.[26]

The publication of the lavish *Monographie de Notre-Dame de Paris et de la nouvelle sacristie* by Viollet-le-Duc and Lassus can be understood against this background. Published sometime between 1857–1860, the monograph promoted the project by making public the drawings of the proposal, and pre-empted any criticism by adding a lengthy "*Notice historique et archéologique*" by the architect-archaeologist M Celtibère.[27] Photographic prints of the cathedral were also included in the publication; the photographic media had now developed and it was possible to make reproducible paper-prints, calotypes, even if this was still an expensive process. Alongside the line drawings of the church plans, sections and elevations, all executed in the precise manner of Viollet-le-Duc's drawing techniques, 12 sharp photographs by the Bisson brothers depict "*l'état actuel*" of the cathedral.[28] This careful documentation in photographs of the state of the cathedral before its restoration follows to the letter the official guidelines for the restoration of religious buildings that Viollet-le-Duc together with Mérimée had drawn up in 1848.[29] Their guidelines strongly recommend photographic documentation of principal views of buildings that are to be restored.[30]

The first plate in the monograph shows, in accordance with the recommendations, a photograph of the cathedral's main facade taken before its restoration: "*Façade principale (l'état actuel)*". The next plate in the monograph shows in contrast the proposed restoration of the same facade drawn in line. Viollet-le-Duc and Lassus here offer the reader a comparison between documented *before* and suggested *after*. The line drawing shows the possibility of making whole while the photograph, specifically by being juxtaposed with the proposed restoration, shows the very incompletion of the cathedral by revealing its missing parts. This fragmentation of the cathedral is highlighted even more in the rest of the photographs that show close-ups of important parts of the building revealing in exquisite detail their crumbling state. The photographs are fully integrated in the monograph, juxtaposed, almost interleaved with the drawings and always presented in the same sized plates.

Some attention has been paid to the role of photography in academic analyses of Viollet-le-Duc's work, although generally the focus has been on the status of his drawings.[31] Lauren M O'Connell points out a direct link between Viollet-le-Duc's drawing activity

Élévation de la Façade Principale.
(Restauration)

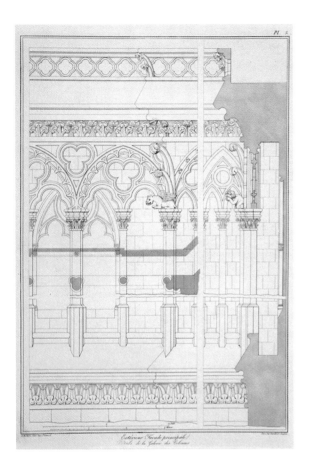

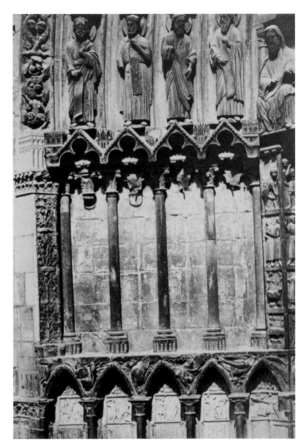

LEFT Notre-Dame, west front, "Exterior" (Extérieure, façade principale). Drawing by Viollet-le-Duc.
Published in *Monographie de Notre-Dame de Paris*, (undated).

RIGHT Notre-Dame, west front, "Detail of the North Door" (Façade principale, détail de la porte, Côté Nord). Photograph by the Bisson brothers, printed by Lemarcier, Paris.
Published in *Monographie de Notre-Dame de Paris*, (undated).

LEFT Notre-Dame,
Fragment of side door
(Fragment du portail
meridional). Photograph
by the Bission brothers,
printed by Lemarcier,
Paris.
Published in *Monographie de
Notre-Dame de Paris*, (undated).

RIGHT Notre-Dame, The
Red Portal (Porte Rouge).
Photograph by the Bission
brothers, printed by
Lemarcier, Paris.
Published in *Monographie de
Notre-Dame de Paris*, (undated).

and photography, noting that his sharp engravings of architectural examples from different parts of the world were often transcribed directly from photographs that he had acquired by various means, a method that helps to explain not only the mass of images produced in Viollet-le-Duc's studio but also the omnipresence of their author.[32] But while O'Connell shows Viollet-le-Duc's innovative use of photography in his studies of architecture, her arguments are framed in terms of a 'collision' between the old media of drawing and the new one of photography. The two media are understood as competing means of representing architecture, one aiming to take the place of the other. By O'Connell's analysis, for Viollet-le-Duc "drawing wins".[33]

While respecting the value of O'Connell's research findings I would like to challenge aspects of her conclusion. It is evident, certainly in the *Monographie de Notre-Dame de Paris*, and in the material that O'Connell herself presents, that the conflict between photography and drawing that she suggests is not present, specifically not in terms of one replacing the other. Rather, one can suggest that drawing and photography, for Viollet-le-Duc, perform two separate functions: the drawing is an instrumental projection that proposes a possible outcome; the photograph on the other hand documents an existing 'now'. Crucially, however, these two functions are performed within the same visual tradition. A closer consideration of the photographs in the *Monographie de Notre-Dame de Paris et de la nouvelle sacristie* shows that they are constructed within the same tradition of representation that directed Viollet-le-Duc's drawing. Despite the novelty of the photographic technique, the Bisson brothers' composition and framing of images conforms to the conventions of architectural representation.

This is obvious for example in the first plate showing the main view of the cathedral. Photographed from a high viewpoint, probably from a building opposite, the linear distortions that would appear had the cathedral been photographed from the ground are reduced. Instead the photograph is framed to create a balanced composition with a great depth of field. One can see, then, that on one side the technique of photography was manipulated to play down the characteristics inherent in the medium (limited depth of focus, distortions of parallels, restrictions of viewpoint) and to reinforce characteristics that bound it to the classical tradition of perspectival architectural drawing. On the other, the viewpoint chosen echoed the development of the tradition of drawing that Viollet-le-Duc himself favoured. In his rhetoric of a scientific study of buildings as objects in whose construction historical evidence might be read, Viollet-le-Duc came to depend on the disembodied abstract viewpoint.

The photographs taken by the Bisson brothers replicate this, removing the camera from the eye level of the general observer on the ground and raising it to an unknown point in space. Indeed one notes that the lifted camera point comes close to the point of view that was favoured by Viollet-le-Duc in his famous hovering perspectives.

This abstraction, in the sense of reducing the presence of the draftsman/photographer, that takes place in both Viollet-le-Duc's and Lassus' drawings and the Bisson brothers' photographic documentation of the cathedral also directs the way in which the context of the cathedral was addressed. In the drawn elevation the main facade of the cathedral is presented as a free-floating projection devoid of all context; even the ground and the adjoining sacristy remain undrawn. The drawing singles out the cathedral as a defined and complete object. This object-like quality is also present in the Bisson brothers' photograph of the west front, albeit that the incompletion of the object, not yet restored, is revealed in the image. Their photograph, or one could call it a photographic portrait, of Notre-Dame is cropped so that the cathedral fills the photographic surface; the cathedral steps out of its urban context, quite an achievement given that the photograph is taken before Baron Haussmann's clearance of the surroundings of Paris' main monuments.

In an intriguing way the photograph foreshadows the physical changes later to effect Notre-Dame's urban setting. In Haussmann's project of *dégagement*, the isolation of major public monuments in the urban landscape, the parvis of the cathedral was hugely enlarged making the cathedral more photogenic. Indeed the buildings that still intrude into the Bisson brothers' photograph of Notre-Dame are precisely the ones which were later to be erased. Here photography works as a projective force, reframing of the building and adumbrating the new task of the cathedral as a historical monument to be visually consumed.[34]

AUTHENTICITY

It is evident, then, that Viollet-le-Duc was familiar with photography from an early stage of its conception and that he advocated its use in architecture, specifically in restoration. In the 1866 article on restoration in the *Dictionnaire* Viollet-le-Duc argues that it is impossible to make too much use of the new medium. "Photography cannot be too sedulously used in restorations."[35] He presents two related reasons for this; one is about the analytical use of photography: "Photography has naturally led architects to be still more scrupulous than before in their respect for the slightest vestiges of an ancient arrangement, and to take more accurate observations of the construction...."[36] Viollet-le-Duc's argument is that photography trains the very ability for the eye to see. The new mechanical means of representing the building exceeded the ability of the human eye: "for very frequently a photograph discovers what had not been perceived in the building itself".[37] To see was for Viollet-le-Duc to know; vision was the absolutely prioritised sense in his theory of architecture, and the analogue between seeing and knowing was direct:

> In fact, while architects possessed only the ordinary means of sketching, even the most exact—the *camera lucida* for example—it was very difficult for them not to make some omissions—not to overlook certain scarcely apparent traces.[38]

The other reason Viollet-le-Duc put forward for the use of photography in restoration is more intriguing. He argues that one crucial advantage of using photography is to offer visual access to knowledge that will be hidden once the restoration is carried out:

> Moreover, when the work of restoration was completed, it was always possible to dispute the correctness of the graphical reports—of what is called the existing state. But photography presents the advantage of supplying indisputable reports—documents which can be permanently consulted when the restorations mask the traces left by the ruin.[39]

Restoration becomes here an inverted form of archaeology in which the knowledge reached by the careful study of the fragments will be used not to lay bare but to cover up the very object of research, the ruin. In its objective of making *whole*, restoration becomes in some sense a destructive force threatening the historical *authenticity* that was the very attraction of the restoration object. However photography steps in here and offers the possibility of seeing behind the mask of restoration. By capturing the 'existing state' the photograph imbricates simultaneously both the past and the future of the monument; it preserves the very 'proofs' which direct the reconstruction that ultimately will veil them. Crucially, then, photography for Viollet-le-Duc will function not just as a means to preserve the ruin but to justify the future of the monument—its reconstruction—that has already occurred.

The implication of this documentation is, that although picturing the transient state of the monument, its ruinous state, photography becomes, in a peculiar way, more permanent than the restored monument itself: "... it [photography] provides them [the architects] with the permanent means of justifying their operation."[40] Through the process of restoration the very authenticity searched for in the object is, curiously, transferred from the building to its documentation. Indeed the photographs are now in one sense the monument while the restored physical structure has become its image.

ORIGIN

Viollet-le-Duc's famous definition of restoration from the *Dictionnaire* demonstrates this effect: "To restore a building is not to preserve it; it is to reinstate it in a condition of completeness which could never have existed at any given time."[41] The breakdown of the logic in the quote—restoration is the act of bringing back something that never existed—opens up a complexity that always marks restoration. In Viollet-le-Duc's aim to define a rational foundation for restoration in the *Dictionnaire* one can note that he was aware of this ambiguity and that he struggled to incorporate it in to his theory. Viollet-le-Duc argues that the objective of restoration is to reconstruct

the "ideal origin" of the building—how it should have been erected and built under ideal circumstances at a specific time in history. According to this theory of restoration history could be grasped through the reconstruction of a series of objects representing its temporal succession. In such a notion of history the identity of the building is equivalent to its origin, the fiction of its instant conception in time rather than to its development in space over time. The historicism that underlay Viollet-le-Duc's restoration theory understands time as the capture of significance instead of as the medium in which the building unfolds. The building is to be restored in order to be historically correct; to represent a particular past moment at the same time as it inevitably inhabits the present.[42]

In the *Dictionnaire* Viollet-le-Duc presents the object for restoration, the thing, as an issue of both excess and loss:

> … we must take note of the many difficulties and obstacles in the way of any authentic restoration. Often buildings or parts of buildings dating from a certain era have been repaired.... Should the unity of style simply be restored without taking account of the later modifications? Or should the edifice be restored exactly as it was, that is, with its original style and later modifications? It is in cases like this that opting absolutely for one or the other of these solutions could be perilous.[43]

In this description the restoration object appears elusive in contrast to the photographs ("documents which can be permanently consulted"); it presents itself as an undefined thing without beginning or end. Restoration, in Viollet-le-Duc's definition, appears not as a problem of the lost building as such, but as the problem of its representation.

SUNDRAWINGS

In 1880 John Ruskin acquired photographic negatives of Amiens Cathedral. He bought them from the photographer M Kaltenbacher, who had previously photographed the cathedral for Viollet-le-Duc. The negatives were obtained to provide illustrations for *The Bible of Amiens*, 1880–1885, the publication in which Ruskin was to use architectural photography most extensively, but the negatives were also acquired with the objective of producing photographs to be commercially sold by Ruskin's agent Mr Ward for four guineas a set.[44] This methodical, practical and even commercial use of photography stands in contrast to the emotional and shifting attitude to the media that Ruskin expressed during his life.[45]

Ruskin was, like Viollet-le-Duc, early in his appreciation of photography; in his autobiography, *Praeteria*, 1885–1889, he even claims to have been one of the first to obtain "sundrawings" in England, sent to him from a friend in France.[46] However while initially embracing it fully, he later became more critical towards the new media, worried mainly by its monochrome nature, but also increasingly suspicious of its mechanical character, which challenged his definition of art as a product created out of human labour.[47] In his *Lectures on Art*, 1870, Ruskin expressed warnings for the use of photography and argued that it had a negative impact on art:

> Let me assure you, once and for all, that photographs supersede no single quality nor use of fine art, and have so much in common with nature, that they even share her temper of parsimony, and will themselves give you nothing valuable that you do not work for. They supersede no good art, for the definition of art is 'Human labour regulated by human design'.[48]

His original enthusiasm for photography arose out of this mechanical aspect, however, and the media's ability to deliver images with minimal involvement of human labour seems to be the very quality that impressed Ruskin deeply in his first contacts with daguerreotypes. In *The Stones of Venice*, 1853, photography is enthusiastically presented as a labour-saving media that would profoundly change the art of engraving:

> A power of obtaining veracity in the representation of material and tangible things, which, within certain limits and conditions is unimpeachable, has now been placed in the hands of all men, almost without labour.[49]

This veracity and efficiency was the aspect of photography that had made Viollet-le-Duc recommend it for use in restoration and it is notable that Ruskin stayed faithful to his idea of a photographic record of endangered buildings even after his first enthusiasm for the photographic technique started to fade. As late as 1871, when he had expressed several doubts about the media, he was in Venice directing the work of photographers, artists and sculptors collecting examples for his St George's Museum at Sheffield. And it was not just Venice that Ruskin 'collected' in daguerreotypes. Ruskin had continuously, since he first began to collect daguerreotypes in Venice in 1845, dispatched assistants to purchase or take photographs of buildings he considered precious and crucially vulnerable.[50]

Ruskin's at first overwhelming enthusiasm for the technical invention, and later more critical stand, must be considered with the knowledge that the photographic media itself transformed to a great extent from its official inauguration in 1839 to 1870, when Ruskin expressed his dismay over photography in his *Lectures on Art*.[51] What in retrospect looks like a smooth uncomplicated process of technical innovation to the photographic media involved a series of complex changes that each brought forth new questions and reservations. With Louis-Jacques-Mandes Daguerre's announcement in 1839 of the 'invention', the daguerreotype entered into the public realm; this was followed by an intense attempt to classify the new media. Photography was awarded

William Henry Fox Talbot
"Photogenic Drawing" of
Queens Collage in Oxford.
Published in William Henry Fox
Talbot, *The Pencil of Nature*, 1844.

an unsettling and provisional status at its inception; being both mechanical and un-authored it appeared to belong neither to nature or culture. This uncertain status of the photograph can be related to the profound crisis of confidence that the concept of nature itself suffered at the time.[52]

As observed by several scholars, in the early nineteenth century the concept of nature inherited from the Enlightenment started to give way to a profoundly different understanding. As part of a gradual process of secularisation, the sacred myths that formed the earliest content of the Western notion of nature began to be displaced by narratives that undermined the religious authority of these mythical structures. The notion of nature as timeless and permanent, created by a single divine act, was slowly undermined by the rising conviction that the earth—and the creatures on it—developed through a history more complex than that of creation, deluge and the retirement of the waters. Nature began to be conceived as a living and active entity that had undergone profound changes since its beginning, and which crucially continued to change. Nature, in short, was understood to have a prolonged and continuous history.

This notion of nature as an entity with a history came to profoundly change the perception of man's position in nature. Acting along with other agents of change in an historical continuum, man started to be seen as a designer effecting the environment. Employing the technologies of drainage, clearing, irrigation, canal building, firing, plant introduction and domestication man altered the historical destiny of the earth.[53] Rather, then, than being God given, stable and harmonious, nature was changing and open to change. By the late eighteenth century nature started to be associated with the irruptive violence of time and this in turn, as Michel Foucault emphasised, conditioned a radical new notion of history and time as synonymous.[54]

The profoundly changed notion of nature, tentatively sketched here, was implicated in the desire to photograph which emerged at the turn of the seventeenth/eighteenth centuries and was underpinned by an objective of rendering permanent the evasive, flickering image of nature as it appeared in the *camera obscura*.[55] Daguerre described his innovative process of fixing the moving images of the *camera obscura* as "the spontaneous reproduction of images of nature" and spoke of the daguerreotype as an "imprint of nature". He went even further and concluded that the daguerreotype was not merely an instrument which served to draw nature but a "chemical and physical process which gives her the power to reproduce herself".[56] Henry Fox Talbot, who parallel to Daguerre refined the methods of rendering permanent the images of the *camera obscura*, similarly defined photography as a natural process, famously calling it "the Pencil of Nature".[57] It is evident from these early comments that the enigma of photography was partly that it appeared to be at once 'natural' and 'mechanical' and that the very absence of 'culture' gave photography a certain 'authenticity' that only nature was thought to own.

Like many of his Victorian contemporaries, Ruskin struggled to reconcile the deductions of natural science with Christian mythology. This problematic runs through his *œuvre*, and is evident particularly in his writing on geology and architecture, where the notion of patina as the "golden stain" complicates history as a concept with beginnings and ends.[58] Ruskin noticeably called his daguerreotypes "sundrawings" and in later years when he was disappointed with the media he still saw a kinship between nature and photography, but then in more negative terms replacing the epithet "sundrawing" with the darker sounding "sunstain".[59] In his warnings about the mechanically passive aspect of the photography quoted earlier, the affinity between nature and photography is maintained but turned into a negative sameness that prevents photography from being art; as nature/technology photography was not a result of "human labour".

THE ORIGINAL

The first daguerreotypes that Ruskin came in contact with were not reproducible, giving them a certain unique relationship to the object photographed.[60] As an 'original' copy, the daguerreotype showed a kinship to the cast, the other method Ruskin used alongside photography and drawing to attain "facts" for his study of Gothic architecture. The calotype, the reproducible paper-print, would later alter this, in some sense, exclusive relationship between copy and object that Ruskin first experienced in the non-reproducible daguerreotypes. By revolutionising the use of photography in publications the calotype would make photographs accessible to a new extent outside the realm of private or institutional collections. This development of photography is reflected in Ruskin's increasingly hesitant attitude. At the same time as photography's technical progress served Ruskin's aim to document endangered Gothic architecture and to spread the knowledge about it through publications, some of the original enigma of photography appears to have been lost with its increasing omnipresence.

Ruskin's criticism of photography has led scholars to assume that his interest in it was of a temporary kind, without significant impact for his aesthetic theory.[61] This assumption is also supported by Ruskin's own account in *Praeterita* where he describes his first encounter with photography as ignorant, not realising its potential danger to art.[62] However, if one looks beyond the debate about photography versus art and considers the role of photography in Ruskin's theory, or rather anti-theory, of restoration, the full impact of the media becomes evident. Ruskin's notion of architectural "effect" and his emphasis on the architectural surface are both informed by his photographic experience. Specifically, the uncertain and tantalising status of photography, as both nature and culture, can be related to the concept of patina that was crucial for Ruskin's condemnation of restoration.

As Fox Talbot had noted in his photographic experiments, patina, the work of nature upon human labour, was picked up in detail by the photographic process. Describing his photograph of Queens College in Oxford he remarked: "This building presents on its surface the most evident marks of the injuries of time and weather, in the abraded state of the stone...."[63] In Ruskin's theory of restoration the authenticity of the monument is guaranteed by these very signs of time rather than by any 'ideal' historical form. This notion of the authentic residing in the weathered surface brought forward Ruskin's argument that restoration was an act of destruction to be forcefully condemned.

THE ENCHANTED LAND

In 1845 Ruskin travelled to Venice; he had briefly visited the city before but this was his first longer stay there. He would keep returning to document it "stone by stone"', but his first attempts left him in despair: "I can find no expedient nor mode of getting at it that will give me what I want... the beauty of it is in the cracks and the stains, and to draw these out is impossible and I am in despair."[64] Photography appeared as the solution to this frustrating drawing experience. In a letter a couple of days later to his father despair is replaced with delight:

> I have been lucky enough to get from a poor Frenchman here, said to be in distress, some most beautiful though very small Daguerreotypes of the palace I have been trying to draw; and certainly Daguerreotypes taken by this vivid sunlight are glorious things... I am very much delighted with these, and I'm going to have more made of pet bits. It is a noble invention—say what they will of it—and any one who has worked and blundered and stammered

as I have done for four days, and then sees the thing he has been trying to do so long in vain done perfectly and faultlessly in half a minute, won't abuse it afterwards.[65]

According to Ruskin's autobiographical account in *Praeteria* it was during his travels in Italy in 1845 that he discovered architecture.[66] In Lucca he was taken by the smoothness and the close fittings of stones in the Medieval buildings and he saw, for the first time, what Medieval builders were and what they meant and "... thereupon literally began the study of architecture".[67] It was also the Italian tour of 1845 that resulted in a change in his approach to drawing. He moved away from the picturesque mode of depiction and what he started to consider to be a superficial concern of making pleasing compositions. When his old master in drawing, the artist Harding, joined him and they travelled together to Venice, the change became evident. Comparing his drawing with Harding's he noted in a letter home:

His sketches are always pretty because he balances their parts together & considers them as pictures—mine are always ugly, for I consider my sketch only as a written note of certain facts, and those I put down in the rudest and clearest way as many as possible. Harding's are all for impression mine are all for information.[68]

The fact that it was on this tour also that Ruskin came to realise the possibilities of the daguerreotype in documenting architecture suggests that Ruskin's 'discovery' of architecture and photography can be seen as interdependent encounters in which the one stimulated the other. The photographic imprints offered something that his own carefully executed studies of the Venetian palaces could not. Their exquisite detailing paired with their minuteness proposed the possibility of a direct relation to the 'original' that was not mediated by the hand of the artist. As Ruskin enthusiastically wrote to his father when he had bought one of his first daguerreotypes: "It is very nearly the same thing as carrying off the palace itself, every chip of stone and stain is there."[69]

The enigmatic attraction of the photographic media lay in its ability to carefully document the decay, the "chip of stone and stain", at the same time as it denied the critical outcome of such disintegration by replacing the reality of the decaying Venice with an intimate world of collection and control. In *Praeterita* nearly 40 years later Ruskin recalled the event:

A French artist producing exquisitely bright small plates which contained, under a lens, the Grand Canal or St Marks Palace as if a magician had reduced the reality to be carried away into an enchanted land. The little gems of picture cost a Napoleon each; but with 200 francs I bought the Grand Canal from the Salute to the Rialto; and packed it away in thoughtless triumph." [70]

The daguerreotype collection gave access to a Venice in miniature; in its accuracy it promised the possibility of a *reunion*, a promise that, however, could never be kept, giving the photography a specifically melancholic character that can be noted in Ruskin's varying attitude to the media.

INSTRUMENT OF CONSERVATION

Ruskin's discovery of architecture on the 1845 tour was accompanied by the acknowledgement that the Gothic architecture he had just started to appreciate was threatened; the buildings were not just crumbling away through neglect and maltreatment but they were, in Ruskin's terms, "vandalised" by "diligent restorers". Writing from Venice in 1845 Ruskin despises the restorers' intervention in saving Venetian palaces:

> You cannot imagine what an unhappy day I spent yesterday before the Casa d'Oro, vainly attempting to draw it while the workmen were hammering it down before my face.... The beauty of the fragments left is beyond all I conceived, & just as I am becoming able to appreciate it, & able to do something that would have kept record of it, to have it destroyed before my face.[71]

Just at the point they were vanishing, Ruskin discovered a visual beauty in the crumbling facades of the Casa d'Oro. The very notion that the palaces were changing, that their weathered surfaces were soon to be replaced with the newly cut stones of the restorer, triggered a desire to record. Ruskin identified the important role the daguerreotype would play in visually 'saving' endangered architectural masterpieces. It offered Ruskin, as it did Viollet-le-Duc, an expedient way of documenting buildings, "... given us, I think, just in time to save some evidence from the great public of wreckers".[72] The very speed of photography suggested that it was possible to hold on to what was in the process of being lost; photography appeared as an instrument of conservation in a world that seemed marked by an overwhelming disintegration. This 'conservative' aspect of photography, I would suggest, explains why Ruskin, who so wholeheartedly despised the new mechanical innovations of the nineteenth century, embraced the media: "Among all the mechanical poison that this terrible nineteenth century has poured upon me, it has given us at any rate one antidote—the Daguerreotype. It's a most blessed invention; that's what it is."[73]

When returning to Venice in 1849 Ruskin brought his own camera to document the buildings of the city with the help of his assistant George Hobbs. During this stay and the following one in 1851 he both made and acquired daguerreotypes. The photographic material was used as the basis for the illustrations drawn for *The Stones of Venice*, 1851–1853, and the accompanying folio *Architectural Examples of Venice*, 1851. The illustrations were drawn with a technique that emphasised shadows and

LEFT Interior of arch, fifth portico, St Mark's, Venice (RF Dag. 7). Daguerreotype.

Ruskin Foundation. Ruskin Library, Lancaster University.

RIGHT South Portico, St Mark's, Venice (RF Dag. 10). Daguerreotype.

Ruskin Foundation. Ruskin Library, Lancaster University.

St Mark's and Ducale
Place, Venice, from the
Piazzetta. (RF Dag. 19).
Daguerreotype.
Ruskin Foundation. Ruskin
Library, Lancaster University.

highlights over outline, mimicking photography to such an extent that, as Ruskin proudly remarked in the foreword to the *Architectural Examples of Venice,* they had been mistaken for daguerreotypes.[74] This method had already been explored in *The Seven Lamps of Architecture*, 1849, where, as Ruskin informed the reader, the plates where: "... either copies of memoranda made upon the spot or enlarged and adapted from Daguerreotypes".[75]

The impact of the daguerreotype on Ruskin's drawing methods has been remarked upon. The favouring of shadow over outline, the cropping of the drawing and attention to detail is without doubt due to his visual experience of the daguerreotype.[76] But here I want to emphasis that there is more to Ruskin's encounter with the daguerreotype than drawing technique. The daguerreotype seems both to suggest and undermine the possibility of a 'true' representation. The simultaneous sharpness and obscurity of photography opens a play between proximity and distance that becomes the driving force in Ruskin's obsessive desire to record the crumbling architecture of Venice down to its minute details. Writing from Padua on his 1845 tour Ruskin tells about a fictional return to the scene of Venice:

> I have been walking all over St Mark's place today, and found a lot of things in the Daguerreotype that I never had noticed in the place itself. It is such a happy thing to be able to depend on everything—to be sure not only that the painter is perfectly honest, but that he can't make a mistake.[77]

The daguerreotype as painter appears to have seen more; it has more attentively been at the *scene*, recording it all without discrimination. In the "sundrawing" nothing was omitted, nothing overlooked out of prejudice or habitual mode of looking. But this sharpness of the camera also makes it uncertain what can be seen, generating a desire to return to the scene to reconfirm the already 'seen'. The very 'realism' of photography sowed a seed of doubt about vision that in Ruskin's study of architecture is turned into a doubt about every aspect of representation.[78]

Writing from Venice in 1852, working on the last parts of *The Stones of Venice*, Ruskin expressed his frustration over his drawing activities:

> And now I have got to such a pitch of fastidiousness that no drawing will satisfy me at all as regards its expression of mere facts—but I must have a Daguerreotype or a cast—and even grumble at those, at the one for exaggerating the shadows— at the other for losing the sharpness of the hollows.[79]

The kinship of photography and cast is proximity, they both *imprint* their object. But in both means of representation Ruskin sees lack—a gap, a loss in translation—

LEFT Detail of facade,
S Michele, Lucca
(RF Dag. 69). Daguerreotype.
Ruskin Foundation. Ruskin
Library, Lancaster University.

RIGHT South side, S Maria
della Spina, Pisa (RF Dag.
62). Daguerreotype.
Ruskin Foundation. Ruskin
Library, Lancaster University.

LEFT Judgment of
Solomon, northwest angle,
Ducal Palace, Venice (RF
Dag. 2). Daguerreotype,
Ruskin Foundation. Ruskin
Library, Lancaster University.

RIGHT Palazzo Bernardo
S Polo, Venice (RF Dag. 24).
Daguerreotype.
Ruskin Foundation. Ruskin
Library, Lancaster University.

that both undermines and directs his documentation of Venice "stone by stone". Ruskin's re-drawing of the daguerreotypes and sketches "made on the spot" aimed to overcome that gap by drawing truthfully, not in the simple sense of realism but with the objective of grasping the "true effect" of architecture; the very visual impact architecture exerted on its beholders.[80] With that objective the exploration into the *topos* of Venice turns into a project in which the process of perception itself becomes in one sense the primary object of vision.

Ruskin's research into the limits of representation in his visual interrogation of Venice points to the crucial difference between his and Viollet-le-Duc's interaction with photography. For Viollet-le-Duc photography charted the critical state of the building and acted to support the restorers' intervention, functioning as a proof that the 'operation' that would bring the building back to 'life' was rightly executed. For Ruskin, on the other hand, photography acted, I would argue, as a catalyst in developing his critical stance to the endeavour of such restoration. Photography was part of forging a new sense of perception and defining visual effects that would challenge the very space in which Viollet-le-Duc's 'operation' took place.

STONE TO STONE

The commercially produced daguerreotypes of Venice from Ruskin's time often show carefully chosen and balanced compositions with a great depth of field; by contrast Ruskin's own daguerreotypes favour close viewpoints that result in unusual cropping and wayward perspectives which undermine the conventional picturesque organisation of the pictorial motif.[81]

When in *The Seven Lamps of Architecture*, 1849, Ruskin makes a plea to the general public to document Medieval architecture by the means of photography he encourages the photographer to ignore any perspectival conventions:

> I would particularly desire to direct the attention of amateur photographers to this task; earnestly requesting them to bear in mind that while a photograph of a landscape is merely an amusing toy, one of early architecture is a precious historical document; and that this architecture should be taken, not merely when it is present itself under picturesque general forms but by stone to stone, and sculpture to sculpture; seizing every opportunity afforded by scaffolding to approach it closely, and putting the camera in any position that will command the sculpture, wholly without regards to the resultant distortions of the vertical lines; such distortions can always be allowed for, if once the details are completely obtained.[82]

The issue here is about coming 'closer', to faithfully record the 'stones' by letting the camera 'touch' every part of the deteriorating architecture. In order to obtain "a precious historical document" Ruskin emphasises that the photographers should act at close range and not miss any opportunity to be *near* their object. Indeed the suggestion that the photographers should not hesitate, in the name of history, to climb the scaffolding, reflects Ruskin's own obsessive activity in ascending architecture: "I have been up all over it [San Michele, Lucca] and on the roof to examine it in detail."[83]

The intimate position of the camera that Ruskin recommends acutely reveals the limitations of geometrical perspective: to obtain the architectural detail in full the amateur photographers are requested to allow unfamiliar linear distortions to enter into the photographic image. Photography here acts to change the relation between observer and object. The distant position from which architecture presents its "picturesque general forms" appears less important than the possibility of interacting with architecture at a near distance, so close in fact that the overall composition is lost and the space of the (depicted) object and the beholder starts to merge.

In *Victorian Photography, Painting and Poetry*, Lindsay Smith identifies a shift from a Romantic to a Victorian account of visual perception. The conventions of the eighteenth century "picturesque" visualisation of landscape give way, during the nineteenth century, to a new emphasis on the optical agency of the spectator.[84] The invention of photography contributed to this shift by altering the understanding of what it meant to 'see'. By revealing perspective as a system rather than a natural visual experience, photography would undermine the dominant role of perspective both as a 'true' model for vision and as a ubiquitous technique for representing three-dimensional space. Smith argues convincingly that Ruskin's persistent inquiry into the visual, his pervasive desire to understand the process of seeing and perceiving evident in *Modern Painters* and *The Stones of Venice*, can be read as a critique of the apparent certainties of a perspectival account of space. Photography, as Smith emphasises, caused Ruskin to continuously re-evaluate the limits of optical fidelity.[85]

Investigating the possibilities of representing the 'seen', Ruskin put forward a more unstable and uncertain model of vision that explored those aspects of space that geometrical perspective failed to address. Indeed in Ruskin's nearsighted observation of the 'stones', one is given a sensation of a space fundamentally different from the geometrical space of perspective. Looking at architecture with Ruskin involves a notion of time and place that fundamentally reconfigures aspects of perspectival vision and its space.

The implication of perspectival vision for the concept of space since its 'rediscovery' in the Renaissance denies any easy summary, but crucial to note is that its subsequent dominance in Western cultures was at the expense of any concept of embodied vision.[86]

The monocular vision of one-point perspective presumed only a static, unblinking eye, an abstract point, in fact, as its privileged beholder. Martin Jay has suggested that this model/presumption led to a visual practise in which the living bodies of both the painter and the viewer were withdrawn, irrevocably divided from that which is to be represented by the screen of the picture plane. In the emptied homogenous space of perspective, Jay suggests, any "specular intertwining" of likenesses between viewer and viewed was surpressed and lost.[87] I want to link Jay's observation to Ruskin's objective to depict architecture *Stone to Stone*.

THE PLEASURE OF THE SURFACE

In a letter to his father from the 1845 tour Ruskin tries to define his desire for drawing architecture:

> There is the strong instinct in me which I cannot analyse to draw and describe the thing I love—not for reputation, nor for the good of others, nor for my own advantage, but a sort of instinct like that for eating or drinking. I should like to draw all St Mark's and all this Verona stone by stone, to eat it all up into my mind, touch by touch.[88]

This ingestion of architecture by a tactile and hungry gaze suggests a fusion of subject and object that challenges the empty and homogeneous space constructed by perspectival vision. The desire to be everywhere, to visually incorporate architecture 'stone by stone' at a close range, makes uncertain the clear cut division between viewer and viewed. The disembodied observing eye of perspectival vision begins in Ruskin's drawing and visual descriptions of architecture to be replaced by a set of tactile, corporeal and desiring eyes.

Ruskin's drawings and descriptions of the disintegrating architecture of Italy divulge a visual pleasure in the study of surfaces; he immerses himself in the weathering surfaces of Gothic architecture and loses himself in the study of its minute details. Architectural surfaces are studied as if they have a depth, a depth however that has nothing to do with the structures of their actual insides but an elusive depth. Searching for its inner character, Ruskin reads the building as a face, watching the cuts and the gaps on the body's surface where the differentiation between the inside and outside of the body are made complicated: "I do with a building as I do with a man, watch the eye and the lips: when they are bright and eloquent, the form of the body is of little consequence."[89]

In this exegesis the surface becomes the location of the building's meaning. Ruskin's strong rejection of restoration and his emphasis on patina is part of a visual argument in which the authenticity is what you *see* not what you know:

Do not let us talk then of restoration. The thing is a Lie from beginning to end. You may make a model of a building as you may of a corpse, and your model may have the shell of the old walls within it as your cast might have the skeleton, with what advantage I neither see nor care: but the old building is destroyed.[90]

Visuality becomes here the argument against restoration at the very same instance as visuality itself is made complex. Ruskin's strong rejection of conservation and his emphasis on the surface as the 'site' of the building is part of an argument that at the same time as it emphasises what you can see—the surface rather than the skeleton—makes that which you see the very thing that disguises. Indeed in Ruskin's argument the truth of the building resides in the veil that shades it, its patina accumulated through age. This, I would argue, points to the significant relationship between Ruskin's emotionally coloured campaign against restoration and his experience of photography.

In *Modern Painters*, 1856, Ruskin writes in capital letters as if to underline his point: "WE NEVER SEE ANYTHING CLEARLY".[91] In the chapter "On Turnerian Mystery" he develops his thoughts on ocular obscurity by drawing a parallel to photography:

... why is it that a photograph always looks clear and sharp—not at all like a Turner? Photographs never look entirely clear and sharp; but because clearness is supposed a merit in them, they are usually taken from [sic] very clearly marked and un-Turnerian subjects: and such results as are misty and faint, though often precisely those which contain the most subtle rendering of nature are thrown away, and the clear ones only are preserved. [92]

The text quoted is part of a longer apology for Turner's controversial paintings that Ruskin passionately defended throughout his life. Ruskin makes a crucial point here that relates to the notion of truth and vision implicated in the study of architecture and his criticism of restoration. The choices of photography and subject, he proposes, are made out of convention, a convention, one can add, inherited largely from the dominant tradition of geometrical perspective. What can be read in Ruskin's comments is the idea that vision is neither neutral nor without history.

Ruskin is in search of transcendental vision beyond the habitual; to see truthfully, to see with an "innocent eye" to use Ruskin's term, means to leave visual convention behind and really *see* the misty and the faint. To see, in one sense, that which obscures clear vision. This will mean the negation of the fiction of a distant spectator, able to see objects in a perspectival space from afar, and replace it with eyes that see with body in context.

BLURRED SPACE

While, as I have pointed out, Viollet-le-Duc's relation to photography was less hesitant than Ruskin's, he also noted that the "indisputable reports" of photography did not always show its object sharply defined. In his lifelong and ambitious project of graphically reconstructing the Mont Blanc mountain range in Switzerland with the same linear sharpness as he graphically reconstructed buildings he came to mistrust the 'reports' the camera delivered:

> I was obliged frequently to revisit the same point of view. In fact a particular direction of the solar rays or a recent fall of snow may enable us to discern clearly at certain moments what had not been visible a few hours before under different aspects. The extreme purity of the air on the heights, while on the one hand it facilitates graphical operations, is, on the other hand, frequently a cause of error, inasmuch as planes of distance widely separated are not distinguishable. It is therefore necessary to wait till the declining sun renders shadows visible that were previously unnoticed, and thus enables us to distinguish these planes of distance. It must also be observed that frequent sojourns on the heights give the eye a power to appreciate the real scale of objects, such as the traveller who visits the altitudes for the first time cannot possess. In this respect drawing always has an advantage over photography, or should at any rate be used to check its results; for photography reproduces the illusions to which the eye is liable amid these solitudes where there is nothing to indicate the scale—since points of comparison are wanting—and where the transparency of the atmosphere almost entirely nullifies aerial perspective.[93]

It is perhaps telling that Viollet-le-Duc chose to dedicate himself so thoroughly to mapping a topography that showed such a resistance to being grasped in a geometrically defined space and whose climatic conditions would constantly challenge Viollet-le-Duc's notion that "to see is to know".[94] When the photographs of the mountain range reproduce the "illusions to which the eye is liable", they lose their cognitive status; the photographs appear to play a trick on vision that makes uncertain both the photograph's documentary performance as well as the cognitive role of vision itself. In the scale-less space of the mountains the eye does not affirm the geometrical knowledge of the mountains' constitution and spatial organisation. Distances become muddled and objects melt together dissolving the very perspectival space in which they are to be mapped, and without which the eye appears no longer to be able to see rightly, the very affluence of light making it see 'illusion'.

In the same way as Viollet-le-Duc's project to capture the *"aspect réel"* of Mont Blanc has to do away with the dazzled eye and replace it with an ideal disembodied eye able to see objects from afar in outline, his theory of restoration was dependent on the idealised gaze of geometrical perspective. In his analytical drawings the architectural

Eugène-Emmanuel
Viollet-le-Duc.
Mont Blanc, Disintegration
of the Chrystalline Rocks.

Published in Eugène-Emmanuel
Viollet-le-Duc, *Mont Blanc,*
a Treatise, 1877.

object is placed in a uniform, infinite space and in his unique hovering perspectives the observer occupies an idealised position outside temporal duration. This abstraction of both space and observer is explored to its limits in Viollet-le-Duc's sections and exploded perspectives in the *Dictionnaire*. Drawn with the objective of showing the inherent logic and functionality of Gothic construction, the opaque depth of "architectural inside" are turned into legible spaces, deciphered with a penetrating gaze that uncovers their inner history. In Viollet-le-Duc's theory of architecture that history corresponds, in each individual constructional detail, to a grander narrative of the nation and the race.

For Viollet-le-Duc, as has been argued above, restoration is the reinforcement of this national history. To restore is to reinstate the monument in its 'ideal' state; this reinstatement will structure the analysis and chronology of the nation's history. This history is narrated in a perspectival space in which the object of knowledge, the monument, is observed by the disincarnated observing eye of geometrical perspective. This ocular distance is maintained in Viollet-le-Duc's elaborate sections where the cutting up of the architectural body is an act of coming closer. Not close in the intimate sense that marks Ruskin's desire to enter the surface of the buildings he observes, but close in order to see more. Put differently, not in order to 'touch' but in order to observe with a gaze that always maintains a distance even when the object is penetrated. This spatial organisation of looking suggests a different relationship between beholder and object than that evident in Ruskin's exploration and enjoyment of architectural surfaces and, I would argue, generates the very different approach evident in Ruskin's and Viollet-le-Duc's theories of restoration.

Guided by the same assumption which structures the visual transparency of geometrical perspective—that all beholders will see the same monument—Viollet-le-Duc's theory of restoration depends on an observer who does not interfere in the narrative. In their idealism the restored architectural structures negated, in the same way as Viollet-le-Duc's hovering perspectives of them, the particular and the unique. By reinstating the ideal state of the monument, a state that, as Viollet-le-Duc suggests never even existed, any individual narrative born out of the local and the specific is parenthesised in favour of one that tells the history of the Nation; its process of development through periods of degeneration and progress.

In Ruskin's study of disintegrating architecture the visual transparency so necessary for Viollet-le-Duc's notion of the monument as an object of decipherable knowledge, becomes clouded. The cool observing eye gives way to an intimate feeling eye that blurs the space separating the viewed from the viewer. In this 'blurred' space, history as master narrative will start to dissolve; reinterpreted and personalised by the beholder it will begin to lose its authority. This loss of the grand narrative will change the notion of the monument from an object of knowledge into one of sentiment, a change that is evident in Viollet-Le-Duc's and Ruskin's shifting approaches to restoration. If Viollet-

Le-Duc can be linked to a tradition of restoration that emerged with the French Revolution, Ruskin's view can be seen to foreshadow the sentimental approach to the monument that would dominate the discourse of conservation during the twentieth century.

For Viollet-le-Duc photography acted as a proof that the monument was authentically restored in the sense of correctly representing a specific instant in history. In this notion, the monument's traditional value of representing immortality was made redundant and replaced by an idea of history in which the monument came to represent time instead of place. Ruskin's experience of the photographic media, on the other hand, made him question the very representation of space that underlay Viollet-le-Duc's historicism. For Ruskin any reconstruction was a threat to an authenticity that resided, not in the building's historical form, but in the very signs of the passage of time that shadowed that form, the patina.

While an archaeological sensitivity connected to an antiquarian approach is already evident, if not satisfyingly resolved, in Viollet-le-Duc's theory, Ruskin's writing suggests a certain indifference to 'history'. Indeed, in his visual theory Ruskin dismantles the notion of history altogether, to replace it with what could be called a "recognition of the past". In the next chapter I will explore further the consequences of Ruskin's notion of the past and reflect on the sentimental approach to the conservation object. It will be suggested that Ruskin's relation to the monument anticipates the popularisation and mass-consumption of heritage. Drawing on Alois Riegl's thesis on the monument expressed in his essay "The Modern Cult of Monuments; Its Character and Its Origin" I will put forward an analysis that rethinks the notion of heritage and its effect on contemporary society. Continuing the spatial theme in the previous chapters I will suggest that the heritage object is inscribed in a field of desire generated by the binary opposition of proximity and distance.

BIBLIOGRAPHICAL SUMMARY

In this chapter the following books have been important in formulating my argument about the interrelationship between photography and restoration:

In the seminal essay on photography, *Camera Lucida*, Roland Barthes noted that "the same century invented History and Photography". Sigfried Kraucauer made a similar reflection in a short essay, called simply "Photography", from 1927, in which he pointed out that historicist thinking emerged at about the same time as did modern photographic technology; historicism, as Kraucauer formulates it, is concerned with "the photography of time". These two essays have helped me to speculate on the notion of historicism in Viollet-le-Duc's restorations and its relation to his photographic experience (Barthes, Roland, *Camera Lucida*, Richard Howard trans., New York: Hill and Wang, 1981; Kraucauer, Siegfried, "Photography", ("Die Photographie", *Frankfurter Zeitung*, 28 October, 1927), Thomas Y Levin trans., *Critical Inquiry*, 19, 1993, pp. 424–425).

Geoffrey Batchen's *Burning with Desire: The Conception of Photography* has been crucial for understanding specifically Ruskin's complex relation to photography, but also for its critical reading of the early history of photography (Batchen, Geoffrey, *Burning with Desire: The Conception of Photography*, Cambridge, MA: MIT Press, 1997). Mark Cousins' essay "Chronography" has been an important help in thinking through aspects of space and time in the photographic media ("Chronography", *Random Walk*, Christian Nicolas, and Eyal Weizman eds., London: Architectural Association, 1998).

Hubert Damisch's *The Origin of Perspective* has been crucial for assimilating the role of perspective in western thought (Damisch, Hubert, *The Origin of Perspective*, Cambridge, MA: MIT Press, 1994), and Martin Jay's *Downcast Eyes* for its criticism of the dominant position of perspective (Jay, Martin, *Downcast Eyes*, Berkeley: University of California Press, 1993). Jonathan Crary's classic *Techniques of the Observer* gave valuable insights into the history of vision in the nineteenth century, and Lindsay Smith's intriguing *Victorian Photography, Painting, and Poetry* helped widen Crary's argument, relating it to Ruskin in particular (Crary, Jonathan, *Techniques of the Observer: On Vision and Modernity in the Nineteenth* Century, Cambridge, MA: MIT Press, 1990; Smith, Lindsay, *Victorian Photography, Painting, and Poetry: The Enigma of Visibility in Ruskin, Morris and the Pre-Raphaelites*, Cambridge: Cambridge University Press, 1995). Jacques Lacan's *Four Fundamental Concepts of Psycho-analysis*, seminars 6, 7 and 8, and *Écrits*, essay 9, have also been crucial for my analysis of Ruskin's daguerreotypes of Venice (*The Four Fundamental Concepts of Psycho-analysis*, Alan Sheridan trans., London: Penguin Books, 1994; *Écrits: a Selection*, trans. Alan Sheridan, Routledge, London, 1997). For the shifting position of nature in western thinking and its relation to technology, Clarence J Glacken's *Traces on the Rhodian Shore* was a useful introduction (Glacken, Clarence J, *Traces on the Rhodian Shore: Nature and Culture in Western Thought from Ancient Times to the End of the Eighteenth Century*, Berkeley: University of California Press, 1967). Above all, Michel Foucault's *The Order of Things* was important for its discursive study of the nature/culture opposition in western thought (Foucault, Michel, *The Order of Things, An Archaeology of the Human Sciences*, (*Les Mots et les choses*, Paris: Gallimard, 1966), New York: Random House, Inc., 1973). Joseph Rykwert's *On Adams House in Paradise* has helped deepen my understanding of the role nature has played in architectural writing and theory as a fantasy of a return to an imaginary origin, (Rykwert, Joseph, *On Adams House in Paradise: The Idea of the Primitive Hut in Architectural History*, New York: The Museum of Modern Art, 1972).

Lauren O'Connell has written at length on Viollet-le-Duc's use of photography, and her article "Viollet-le-Duc on Drawing, Photography and the 'Space Outside the Frame'" provided a useful foil for my argument (O'Connell, Lauren, M, "Viollet-le-Duc on Drawing, Photography and the 'Space Outside the Frame'", *History of Photography*, Vol. 22, No. 2, summer, 1998, pp. 139–145). Other scholars that have written on Viollet-le-Duc's use of photography include: Bergdoll, Barry, "A Matter of Time: Architects and Photographers in Second Empire France" in *The Photographs of Édouard Baldus*, Malcolm Daniel ed., The Metropolitan Museum of Art, New York, 1994; Christ, Yvan, *L'Age d'or de la Photographie*, Paris: Vincent, Fréal et Cie, 1965.

The writing on Ruskin and photography is more extensive. The most intriguing research into the role of photography for Ruskin's aesthetic theory has been carried out by Lindsay Smith in her study *Victorian Photography, Painting, and Poetry*. Smith's argument has informed this chapter's study of the interdependency between photography and restoration (Smith, Lindsay, *Victorian Photography, Painting, and Poetry, The Enigma of Visibility in Ruskin, Morris and the Pre-Raphaelites*, Cambridge: Cambridge University Press, 1995). Other scholars writing on photography and Ruskin include: Bann, Stephen, *The Clothing of Clio: A Study of the Representation of History in Nineteenth-century Britain and France*, Cambridge: Cambridge University Press, 1984; Burns, Karen, "Topographies of Tourism: Documentary Photography and *The Stones of Venice*", *Assemblage*, 32, 1997, pp. 22–44; *I Dagherrotipi Della Collezione Ruskin*, Paolo, Costantini and Italo Zannier eds., Venezia, Alinari, Firenze e Arsenale, 1986; Clegg, Jeanne, and Paul

Tucker, *Ruskin and Tuscany*, Ruskin Gallery in Sheffield, Collection of the Guild of St George in association with Lund Humphries, London: Lund Humphries 1993; Elwall, Robert, *Photography Takes Command: The Camera and British Architecture 1890–39*, Catalogue, London: Heinz Gallery, 1994; Hanson, Brian, "Carrying off the Grand Canal: Ruskin's Architectural Drawings and the Daguerreotype", *The Architectural Review*, Feb. 1981, pp. 104–109; Harvey, Michael, "Ruskin and Photography", *The Oxford Art Journal*, 7:2, 1985, pp. 25–33; Haslam, Ray, "'For the Sake of the Subject': Ruskin and the Tradition of Architectural Illustration", *The Lamp of Memory, Ruskin, Tradition and Architecture*, Michael Wheeler and Nigel Whiteley eds., Manchester: Manchester University Press, 1992.

Parts of this chapter have been published in an earlier version as *Ruskin's Daguerreotypes in Venice*, Proceedings of the Nordic Conference for Advanced Studies in Cultural Studies, Linköping University Electronic Press 2005.

PRIMARY SOURCES

Viollet-le-Duc, Eugène-Emmanuel:

Dictionnaire raisonné de l'architecture française du XIe au XVIe siècle, Paris: B Bance, A Morel, 10 Vols., 1854–1868, 1867–1889. Hereafter referred to as *Dictionnaire*.

On Restoration trans. B Bucknall, Sampson Low, Marston, Low, and Searle, London, 1875, p. 1. From chapter "Restauration", in Viollet-le-Duc, Eugène-Emmanuel, *Dictionnaire raisonné de l'architecture française du XIe au XVIe siècle*, Paris: B Bance, A Morel, Vol. 8, 1866. Hereafter referred to as *On Restoration*.

Monographie de Notre-Dame de Paris et de la nouvelle sacristie, with Lassus, Jean Baptiste Antoine, Paris (undated).

Cités et ruines américaines: Mitla, Palenqué, Izamal, Chichen Itza, Uzmal; Photographs by Désiré Charnay, Paris: 1863.

Le Massif du Mont Blanc; Etude sur sa constitution géodésique et géologique sur les Transformations et sur l'état ancien et moderne de ses glaciers, Paris: Libraire Polytechnique J Braudry, 1876. Translated as *Mont Blanc, a Treatise*, B Bucknall trans., London: Sampson Low, Marston, Searle, and Rivington, 1877.

Histoire d'un dessinateur: Comment on apprend à dessiner, Paris: J Hetzel, 1879. Translated as *Learning to Draw or the Story of a Young Designer*, New York: Putman, 1881.

Ruskin, John:

The Complete Works of John Ruskin, ET Cook and Alexander Wedderburn eds., London: George Allan, 39 Vols., 1903–1912. Hereafter referred to as *Works*.

The Seven Lamps of Architecture, Kent: George Allan, 2nd ed., 1880, Appendix I.

Examples of the Architecture of Venice, Sketched and Drawn to Measurement from the Edifices, Sixteen plates with descriptions, London: Smith, Elder & Co., 3 Vols., 1851.

Unpublished material:

John Ruskin's collection of Daguerreotypes, Previously the Bembridge Collection, now in the Ruskin Foundation held in the Ruskin Library, Lancaster University, England. Since I visited this collection in 2001 extensive work has been made in re-cataloguing and exhibiting the Ruskin Daguerreotypes and part of the material is now published.

NOTES

1 The full title of Pugin's book was: *Contrasts, or, A parallel between the noble edifices of the fourteenth and fifteenth centuries, and similar buildings of the present day; showing the present decay of taste*, printed and published by the author, London, 1836.

2 For the history of the *Mission Héliographique* see, Malcolm, Daniel, "Édouard Baldus, Artist Photographer" in *The Photographs of Édouard Baldus*, New York: The Metropolitan Museum of Art, 1994, p. 105; and Bergdoll, Barry, "A Matter of Time: Architects and Photographers in Second Empire France", in the same publication, pp. 106–108.

3 Elwall, Robert, *Photography Takes Command: The Camera and British Architecture 1890-39*, (exhibition catalogue), London: Heinz Gallery, 1994.

4 Viollet-le-Duc, Eugène-Emmanuel, *On Restoration*, p. 1 and Ruskin, John, letter to WH Harrison, 12 August, 1846, *Works*, Vol. 3, p. 210, n. 2.

5 See for example: Pevsner, Nikolaus, "Scrape and anti-scrape", in *The Future of the Past. Attitudes to conservation 1174–1974*, Jane Fawcett ed., London: Thames & Hudson, 1976; Kåring, Göran, *När medeltidens sol gått ned*, Stockholm: Kungl. Vitterhets Historie och Antikvitets Akademien 1992; Choay, Françoise, *L'Allégorie du Patrimoine*, Paris: Seuil, 1992; Jokilehto, Jukka, *A History of Architectural Conservation*, Oxford: Butterworth-Heinemann, 1999.

6 Pevsner, Nikolaus, *Ruskin and Viollet-le-Duc, Englishness and Frenchness in the Appreciation of Gothic Architecture*, London: Thames & Hudson, 1969.

7 The end of the eighteenth century and the beginning of nineteenth century saw for example the publication of Quatremère de Quincy's *Dictionnaire d'architecture*, 3 Vols., part of the *Encyclopédie méthodique*, Panckoucke ed., Paris: 1788–1825; Jacques Guillaume Legrand's *Essai sur l'histoire générale de l'architecture*, Paris: 1809; and Jean Baptiste Seroux d'Agincourt's *Histoire de l'art par les monumens*, Paris: Treuttel et Würtz, 1823.

8 Viollet-le-Duc, Eugène-Emmanuel, *Dictionnaire raisonné de l'architecture française du XIe au XVIe siècle*, Paris: B Bance, A Morel, 10 vols., 1854–1868. Hereafter referred to as *Dictionnaire*.

9 See Bergdoll, Barry, "The Legacy of Viollet-le-Duc's Drawings", *Architectural Record*, 169:11, 1981, p. 66.

10 See Barry Bergdoll's introduction to Viollet-le-Duc, "The Dictionnaire raisonné of Viollet-le-Duc", in Eugène Emmanuel, *The Foundation of Architecture: Selections from the 'Dictionnaire raisonné'*, New York:

Braziller, 1990, pp. 1–30. For a thorough presentation of Quatremère de Quincy's theories of architecture see Lavin, Sylvia, *Quatremère de Quincy and the Invention of a Modern Language of Architecture*, Cambridge, MA: MIT Press, 1992.

11 Viollet-le-Duc, Eugène-Emmanuel, *On Restoration*, pp. 13–14.

12 For Viollet-le-Duc's notion of construction and its crucial role in his theory of architecture see Bergdoll in Eugène Emmanuel, *The Foundation of Architecture*, pp. 1–30, and Martin Bressani, "The Life of Stones: Viollet-le-Duc's Physiology of Architecture", *ANY: Architecture New York*, No. 14, 1996, pp. 23–27.

13 For Viollet-le-Duc's notion of the relation between construction and the history of architecture see, Mårtelius, Johan, *Göra Arkitekturen Historisk: om 1800-talets arkitekturtänkande och I G Clasons Nordiska museum*, Stockholm: Arkitektur Museet, 1987, pp. 50–56.

14 Etlin, Richard A, *Frank Lloyd Wright and Le Corbusier: The Romantic Legacy*, Manchester and New York: Manchester University Press, 1994, pp. 4–8 and 47.

15 For Viollet-le-Duc's role in the *Commission des monuments historiques* see Kevin D Murphy, *Memory and Modernity, Viollet-le-Duc at Vézelay*, Pennsylvania: Pennsylvania State University Press, 2000.

16 See Malcolm and Bergdoll in *The Photographs of Édouard Baldus* p. 105 and pp. 106–108.

17 McCauley, Elizabeth, *Industrial Madness, Commercial Photography in Paris, 1848–71*, New Haven: Yale University Press, 1994, p. 309 and 411, note 23.

18 Kevin Murphy has shown that the transformation of the Church of Sainte-Madeleine in Vézelay from a local church into a national historical monument was driven by conflicts. The local society protested mostly in vain against the radical transformation their church underwent with Viollet-le-Duc's restoration. The local support for the project is, however, equally interesting. Arguments were proposed that the very restoration of the church would benefit local society by bringing new visitors into the town, an argument that can still be heard in favour of expensive restorations today; the close-knit relationship between tourism and conservation is not a new phenomenon. See Murphy, Kevin D, *Memory and Modernity: Viollet-le-Duc at Vézelay*, Pennsylvania: Pennsylvania State University Press, 2000, pp. 38–53 and pp. 135–148.

19 "... que pour se frayer un chemin dans l'avenir, il faut savoir d'où l'on vient", Viollet-le-Duc, Eugène-Emmanuel, *Dictionnaire*, Vol. 1, 1854, p. vi.

20 Viollet-le-Duc, Eugène-Emmanuel, *Dictionnaire*, Vol. 1, 1854, pp. vi–vii.

21 Viollet-le-Duc, Eugène-Emmanuel, *On Restoration*, p. 15.

22 "Il semble que les découvertes nouvelles viennent en aide à ce mouvement général. Au moment où la main des artistes ne suffit pas à recueillir les restes si nombreux et si précieux de nos édifices anciens, apparaît la photographie, qui forme en quelques années un inventaire fidèle de tous ces débris", Viollet-le-Duc, Eugène-Emmanuel, *Dictionnaire*, Vol. 1, 1854, p. vii.

23 The first photographic documentation of the cathedral ordered by Viollet-le-Duc consisted of daguerreotypes by Kruines and Lerbours that somewhat ironically appear to have been lost. See further Christ, Yvan, *L'Âge d'or de la Photographie*, Paris: Vincent, Fréal et Cie, 1965, p. 15.

24 For the history of the restoration of Notre-Dame see Reiff, DD, "Viollet-le-Duc and Historical Restoration: The West Portal of Notre-Dame", *Journal of Architectural Historians*, Vol. 30, No. 1, March, 1971, pp. 17–30. See also Christ, Yvan, *L'Âge d'or de la Photographie*, Paris: Vincent, Fréal et Cie, 1965, p. 15, and Bergdoll, in *The Photographs of Édouard Baldus*, pp. 106–108.

25 For example the *Monographie de Notre-Dame de Paris et de la nouvelle sacristie*, by Jean Baptiste Antoine Lassus and Eugène Emmanuel Viollet-le-Duc was bought or donated to the Royal Library in Stockholm in 1853.

26 Murphy, Kevin D, *Memory and Modernity: Viollet-le-Duc at Vézelay*, Pennsylvania: Pennsylvania State University Press, 2000, pp. 144–148.

27 Lassus, Jean Baptiste Antoine and Viollet-le-Duc, Eugène Emmanuel, *Monographie de Notre-Dame de Paris et de la nouvelle sacristie*, Paris [undated].

28 Lassus, Jean Baptiste Antoine and Viollet-le-Duc, Eugène Emmanuel, *Monographie de Notre-Dame de Paris et de la nouvelle sacristie*, Paris [undated].

29 For the Service des Edifices Diocésain, a division of Ministry of Education and Religion responsible for the control of the restoration of religious buildings, see Bergdoll in *The Photographs of Édouard Baldus*, p. 105.

30 Barry Bergdoll has pointed out that this was the first systematic use of photography in restoration in *The Photographs of Édouard Baldus*, p. 105.

31 See for example Bergdoll, *Architectural Record*, 169:11, 1981, pp. 63–67, and *The Foundation of Architecture*. See also Boudon, Françoise, "Le réel et l'imaginaire chez Viollet-le-Duc: les figures du Dictionnaire de l'architecture", *Revue de l'art*, 58/59, 1983, pp. 95–114; Durant, Stuart, "Nulla Dies sine Linea": Viollet-le-Duc's Drawings" in *Eugène-Emmanuel Viollet-le-Duc, 1814–79*, London: Academy Éditions, 1980.

32 Lauren O'Connell has pointed out, for example, that in 1877 Viollet-le-Duc wrote and illustrated *L'Art Russe* without ever visiting Russia. His knowledge of 'Russian' architecture was drawn to a large extent from photographs sent to him from the commissioner of the book, Viktor Butovsky, the Director of the Museum of Art and Industry in Moscow. Moreover as O'Connell has shown convincingly, there exists a correspondence between these photographs and the specific plates in the *L'Art Russe*, see O'Connell, Lauren, M "Viollet-le-Duc on Drawing, Photography and the 'Space Outside the Frame'", *History of Photography*, Vol. 22, No. 2, summer, 1998, pp. 139–141.

33 O'Connell, *History of Photography*, p. 145.

34 For a discussion on photography and its role in the reconfiguration of Paris see Shelley Rice, *Parisian Views*, Cambridge MA, London: MIT Press, 1997.

35 Viollet-le-Duc, Eugène-Emmanuel, *On Restoration*, p. 69.

36 Viollet-le-Duc, *On Restoration*, p. 68.

37 Viollet-le-Duc, *On Restoration*, p. 69. In the newer translation a slightly different emphasis appears "for very often one discovers on a photographic proof some feature that went unnoticed on the building itself", Viollet-le-Duc, *The Foundation of Architecture*, p. 225.

38 Viollet-le-Duc, *On Restoration*, p. 68.

39 Viollet-le-Duc, *On Restoration*, p. 68.

40 Viollet-le-Duc, *On Restoration*, p. 69.

41 Viollet-le-Duc, *On Restoration*, p. 9.

42 The complexities of this argument are significant, for inevitably the notion of history implied by Viollet-le-Duc is made up of a sequence of such fictional moments of origin that, by definition, can only be constructed in the present. To be authentic, the ancient building has to occupy a specific slot in this temporal continuum that constitutes history, thus the building's authenticity is also mortgaged to the now, rather than the then. See Vinegar, Aaron, "Viollet-le-

Duc and Restoration in the Future Anterior", *Future Anterior*, Vol. III, No. 2, 2006, pp. 55–65.

43 Viollet-le-Duc, *The Foundation of Architecture*, p. 210.

44 See Ruskin, John, *Works*, Vol. 33, p. 13 (The Bible of Amiens).

45 See Ruskin, *Works*, Vol. 3, p. 210, n. 2 (letter to father from Venice, 7 October, 1845); Vol. 11, pp. 199, 201–202, 312 ("The Stones of Venice", 1853); Vol. 19, p. 89 ("The Cestus of Agalia", 1865); Vol. 19, p. 150 ("The Cestus of Agalia", 1865); Vol. 20, p. 165 ("Lectures on Art", 6: Light, 1870); Vol. 14, pp. 357–359 ("The Black Arts: A Reverie in the Strand", 1887); Vol. 35, pp. 372–373 ("Praeteria", 1886–89).

46 See Ruskin, *Works*, Vol. 35, pp. 372–373 ("Praeteria", 1886–89); Michael Harvey has noted that Ruskin's claim to be the first to obtain daguerreotypes in Britain is obscured by the date referred to. Ruskin claims to have seen them in "my last days at Oxford", i.e. during 1841. Already in March 1840, however, daguerreotypes had been exhibited at the Royal Society. Nevertheless, the claim is interesting in itself in that it confirms the impact photography asserted on Ruskin in either positive or negative terms. See further Harvey, Michael, "Ruskin and Photography", *The Oxford Art Journal*, 7:2, 1985, pp. 25–33.

47 See for example "The Black Art: A Reverie in the Strand", 1887, and "Lectures on Art, 6: Light", 1870, in Ruskin, *Works*, Vol. 14, pp. 357–59 and Vol. 20, p. 165.

48 Ruskin, *Works*, Vol. 20, p. 165.

49 Ruskin, *Works*, Vol. 11, p. 199.

50 This is underlined by Michael Harvey in his article "Ruskin and Photography", *The Oxford Art Journal*, 7:2, 1985, p. 26.

51 Ruskin, *Works*, Vol. 20, p. 165.

52 In his intriguing and highly rewarding analysis of the conception of photography Geoffrey Batchen has highlighted the unsettled and provisional status photography was afforded at its inception, not clearly belonging to either nature or culture. See Batchen, Geoffrey, *Burning with Desire, the Conception of Photography*, Cambridge, MA: MIT Press, 1997, pp. 62–69.

53 I refer here to Clarence J Glacken's reading of Count Buffon's *Des Époques de la Nature*, 1780. See Glacken, Clarence J, *Traces on the Rhodian Shore: Nature and Culture in Western Thought from Ancient Times to the End*

of the Eighteenth Century, Berkeley and Los Angelos: University of California Press, 1967, pp. 655–705. See specifically Foucault's argument on the formation of the scientific discipline of natural history, Chapter 5, "Classifying", in Foucault, Michel, *The Order of Things: An Archaeology of the Human Sciences*, New York: Random House, Inc., 1971, pp. 125–165.

54 Foucault, *The Order of Things*, pp. 125–165.

55 Batchen, *Burning with Desire*, pp. 62–69.

56 See Daguerre, Louis-Jacques-Mandes, "Daguerreotype", in *Classic Essays on Photography*, Alan Trachtenberg ed., New Haven: Leete's Island Books, 1980.

57 Talbot, William Henry Fox, *The Pencil of Nature*, (Brief historical sketch of the invention of the art), London: Longman & Co., 1844. Reprinted as H Fox Talbot's *The Pencil of Nature, anniversary facsimile*, New York: Larry J Schaaf, Kraus, 1989.

58 On Ruskin and geological time see further Arrhenius, Thordis, "The pleasure of the Surface" in *Jorge Otero-Pailos: The Ethics of Dust*, Eva Ebersberger and Daniela Zyman eds., Thyssen-Bornemisza Art Contemporary, Walther König Verlag der Buchhandlung, 2009.

59 Ruskin, *Works*, Vol. 5, p. 40.

60 In her suggestive article "Topographies of Tourism: Documentary Photography and The Stones of Venice", Karen Burns highlights this intimate relationship that the daguerreotypes established not least through their limited size and reflective surfaces. See Burns, Karen, "Topographies of Tourism: Documentary Photography and The Stones of Venice", *Assemblage*, 32, 1997, pp. 22–44.

61 See Hanson, Brian, "Carrying off the Grand Canal: Ruskin's Architectural Drawings and the Daguerreotype", *The Architectural Review*, February 1981, pp. 104–109; and Harvey, Michael, "Ruskin and Photography", *The Oxford Art Journal*, 7:2, 1985, pp. 25–33. A different opinion is held by Lindsay Smith who has clearly shown the lasting and fundamental impact of photography on Ruskin's aesthetic theories. See Smith, Lindsay, *Victorian Photography, Painting, and Poetry, The Enigma of Visibility in Ruskin, Morris and the Pre-Raphaelites*, Cambridge: Cambridge University Press, 1995.

62 Ruskin, *Works*, Vol. 35, pp. 372–373.

63 Talbot, *The Pencil of Nature*, London: Longman, Brown, Green & Longman, 1844. *The Pencil of Nature* was published in six parts between June 1844 and April

1845 containing a total of 24 photographs. The quote is from the facsimile of Leopoldo II, Grand Duca di Toscana, which copy contains only plates 1–5, reprinted in 1976 by Mycron, Firenze. Another facsimile is published by Larry J Schaaf, Kraus 1989, containing all 24 photographs. See H Fox Talbot's *The Pencil of Nature, anniversary facsimile*, New York: Larry J Schaaf, Kraus, 1989.

64 Shapiro, Harold L, *Ruskin in Italy: Letters to his Parents*, 1845, Oxford: Clarendon Press, 1972, letter No. 139, p. 218.

65 Ruskin, *Works*, Vol. 3, p. 210, n. 2 (letter to father from Venice, 7 October, 1845); see also Shapiro, ed., *Ruskin in Italy: Letters to his Parents 1845*, letter No. 142, p. 220.

66 Ruskin, *Works*, Vol. 35, p. 350.

67 Bradley, John Lewis, ed., *Ruskin's Letters from Venice, 1851–52*, New Haven: Yale University Press, 1955, p. 180.

68 Shapiro, *Ruskin in Italy*, letter No. 142, p. 220.

69 Shapiro, *Ruskin in Italy*, letter No. 142, p. 220.

70 Ruskin, *Works*, Vol. 35, pp. 372–373.

71 Shapiro, *Ruskin in Italy*, letter No. 130, p. 209.

72 Ruskin, *Works*, Vol. 3, p. 210, n. 2 (letter to WH Harrison, 12 August, 1846).

73 Shapiro, *Ruskin in Italy*, letter No. 149, pp. 224–225.

74 Ruskin, John, *Examples of the Architecture of Venice, Sketched and Drawn to Measurement from the Edifices, Sixteen plates with descriptions*, London: Smith, Elder & Co., 1851, "Preface" to Vol. 1. See also Harvey, Michael, "Ruskin and Photography", *The Oxford Art Journal*, 7:2, 1985, p. 25–33.

75 Ruskin, *Works*, Vol. 8, p. 4.

76 In his article "Carrying off the Grand Canal: Ruskin's Architectural Drawings and the Daguerreotype", *The Architectural Review*, February, 1981, pp. 104–109, Brian Hanson traced several examples where the illustrations by Ruskin's hand can be linked to specific daguerreotypes in his photographic collection. See also Haslam, Ray, "'For the Sake of the Subject' Ruskin and the Tradition of Architectural Illustration", in *The Lamp of Memory: Ruskin, Tradition and Architecture*, Michael Wheeler and Nigel Whiteley eds., Manchester: Manchester University Press, 1992.

77 Shapiro, *Ruskin in Italy*, letter No. 149, pp. 224–225.

78 See Hanson, "Carrying off the Grand Canal: Ruskin's Architectural Drawings and the Daguerreotype", *The Architectural Review*, p. 107.

79 Bradley, *Ruskin's Letters from Venice, 1851–52*, letter 256, p. 297. See also Ruskin, *Works*, Vol. 10, pp. 466–467, and Vol. 8, p. 13 on the importance of the cast.

80 See John Ruskin's comments on effects in the preface to *Examples of the Architecture of Venice, Sketched and Drawn to Measurement from the Edifices, Sixteen plates with descriptions*, London: Smith, Elder & Co., 1851, Vol. 1.

81 Hanson has suggested that there exists a noticeable difference in composition between the first daguerreotypes that Ruskin acquired and the daguerreotypes he himself ordered to be taken. However in Ruskin's collection of daguerreotypes held in the Ruskin Library, Lancaster University, it is difficult to distinguish between the commercially bought daguerreotypes and the later commissioned ones. The daguerreotypes are not dated and cannot with any certainty be linked to Ruskin's own catalogue of daguerreotypes (which do not indicate date of acquisition). See further Hanson, "Carrying off the Grand Canal", *The Architectural Review*, p. 104.

82 Ruskin, John, *The Seven Lamps of Architecture*, 2nd ed. George Allan, Kent, 1880, Appendix I. In the preface to the first edition of *The Seven Lamps of Architecture*, this plea for photographing Gothic architecture is also included, in that case with a specific reference to Notre-Dame. See Ruskin, *Works*, Vol. 8, p. 13.

83 Shapiro, *Ruskin in Italy*, letter No. 26, p. 54.

84 Smith, *Victorian Photography, Painting, and Poetry*, p. 19.

85 Smith, *Victorian Photography, Painting, and Poetry*, pp. 18–52.

86 For a history of perspective see foremost Hubert Damisch's *The Origin of Perspective*, Cambridge, MA: MIT Press, 1994. In relation to the argument of a disembodied vision see Merleau-Ponty, Maurice, *The Visible and the Invisible*, Claude Lefort ed., Alphonso Lingis trans., Evanston: Northwestern University Press, 1968 and also specifically Jacques Lacan's critique of Merleau-Ponty's argument in *The Four Fundamental Concepts of Psycho-analysis*, Alan Sheridan trans., London: Penguin Books, 1994, seminar 6 and 7 pp. 67–90.

87 Jay, Martin, *Downcast Eyes*, Berkeley: University of California Press, 1993, p. 55.

88 Ruskin, *Works*, Vol. 10, p. xxv (letter to father from Verona 2 June, 1852).

89 Ruskin, *Works*, Vol. 12, p. 89. Ruskin's emphasis on the surface of the body can be read against Jacques Lacan's analysis of the erogenous zones of the body: the lips, eyelids, mouth, etc.. Lacan suggests that these cuts or apertures allow the sense of edge, borders or margins by differentiating the body from the organic functions associated with such apertures. Because they are described as being on the very surface of the subject they have no specular image, no "outside" that they represent. It is this which enables them to be "the 'stuff', or rather the lining… [of] the very subject that one takes to be the subject of consciousness". See Lacan, Jacques, *Écrits: A Selection*, London: Routledge, 1997, pp. 314–315.

90 Ruskin, *Works*, Vol. 8, p. 242.

91 Ruskin, *Works*, Vol. 6, p. 75: "there is a continual mystery caused throughout all spaces, caused by the absolute infinity of things. WE NEVER SEE ANYTHING CLEARLY." (original emphasis).

92 Ruskin, *Works*, Vol. 6, pp. 81–82. See also Smith, *Victorian Photography, Painting, and Poetry*, p. 202.

93 Viollet-Le-Duc, Eugène-Emmanuel, *Mont Blanc, a Treatise, (Le Massif du Mont Blanc; Etude sur sa constitution géodésique et géologique sur les Transformations et sur l'état ancien et moderne de ses glaciers*, Paris: Libraire Polytechnique, J Braudry, 1876) B Bucknall trans., London: Sampson Low, Marston, Searle, and Rivington, London, 1877, pp. 6–7.

94 Viollet-Le-Duc, Eugène-Emmanuel, *Histoire d'un dessinateur: Comment on apprend à dessiner*, Paris: J Hetzel, 1879. Translated as *Learning to Draw or the Story of a Young Designer*, New York: Putman, 1881, p. 68.

THE MODERN CULT OF MONUMENTS

The Austrian art historian Alois Riegl's essay "The Modern Cult of Monuments: Its Character and Its Origin" makes an unprecedented attempt to speculate on the popularisation of heritage in Western culture.[1] His 1903 essay remains fascinating as it predicts the imminent emergence of a ubiquitous admiration for the old, while putting forward an intriguing proposal for how this "cult" of the old would affect the notion of the "monument". Intriguingly, Riegl identified age as the clue to the extension of heritage into mass culture. Age, signified through disintegration, manifested itself immediately to the beholder; no scientific or art historical knowledge was needed to appreciate its visual qualities. Riegl saw this visual directness as the future potential of age in a mass society directed by moods and feelings, what he called "*Stimmung*", rather than rational thinking. A review of Riegl's groundbreaking essay and its speculations about the monument highlights contradictions and complexities that mark the discourse and practice of conservation, and provides a unique perspective on the deep structures organising the desire for the past more than a century later. Written in 1903, as an introductory text to a new law regarding historical preservation, Riegl's essay suggested a new classification system for monuments based on the values attributed to them—commemorative-value, age-value and historical-value are examples. In Riegl's visually orientated analysis the gaze of the beholder was prioritised, and the values defining the monument were identified according to the effect they generated upon the subject.

Riegl's argument has been central for much of the analysis made in this book, and specifically his notion of age-value becomes crucial in the later chapters' discussion of the expansion of the monument and its final development into a mass cult in the twenty-first century. Riegl's analysis makes it clear that the cult of old objects in modern society is dependent on their remoteness and yet that the meeting between an observer and an historical object transgresses that distance. My reading of Riegl's essay will pay attention to this spatial aspect of Riegl's argument suggesting that an intriguing play of proximity and distance forms a tension between the 'pastness' of the monument and its newness that forms the very core in the modern cult of monuments.[2]

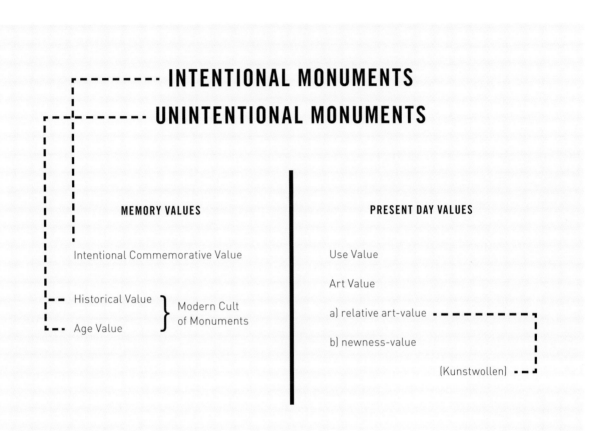

INTENTIONAL MONUMENTS
UNINTENTIONAL MONUMENTS

MEMORY VALUES

Intentional Commemorative Value

Historical Value
Age Value

} Modern Cult
of Monuments

PRESENT DAY VALUES

Use Value

Art Value

a) relative art-value

b) newness-value

(Kunstwollen)

Diagram of relationships
between various types
of memory-values and
present-day-values from
Alois Riegl's "The Modern
Cult of Monument: its
Character and its Origin,"
1903. Drawn by author.

THE RECEPTION OF THE MODERN CULT OF MONUMENTS

The Modern Cult of Monuments: Its Character and Its Origin was written just before Riegl's early death at the age of 47. In comparison to his three seminal works, *Problems of Style*, 1897, *Late Roman Art Industry*, 1901, and *The Group Portraiture of Holland*, 1902, it has achieved limited interest from scholars in art theory.[3] Within the field of architectural conservation, however, it is acknowledged as a central text. This applies specifically to the period of the 1980s that saw a revived interest in history in architecture. Generally, conservation scholars praise Riegl's essay for its clear discrimination between conflicting values involved in historical preservation. However, these writers tend to miss the challenge Riegl's essay poses to the very object of conservation: the monument.[4]

Riegl wrote before the two World Wars whose massive material destruction would acutely change both the practice and discourse of conservation. His theory, then, was formulated before the trauma of the Holocaust that has so strongly directed our contemporary thinking about the monument; neither did Riegl live to see the renaissance of the monument as an instrument of power in the post-war totalitarian states.[5] However, despite its formulation within a particular and bounded historical context, Riegl's analysis can still contribute to deepen the understanding of the phenomena of conservation. Riegl identified a function for the monument in modern society that went beyond its documentary value as history to the emotional force of the old itself. Age was the clue to the extension of heritage into mass culture: "Age-value manifests itself immediately through visual perception and appeals directly to our emotions. To be sure, the scientific basis of historical value originally gave rise to age-value but in the end age-value conveys the achievements of scholarship to everyone...."[6] No scientific or art historical knowledge was needed to appreciate the visual qualities of age. This directness was the future potential of age in a mass society directed, as Riegl saw it, by moods and feelings, *Stimmung*, rather than rational thinking. Examining "The Modern Cult of Monuments" in some detail, specifically addressing Riegl's concepts of intentional (*gewollte*) and unintentional (*ungewollte*) monuments, shows how Riegl's analysis anticipated the effect of a 'cult of monuments' in contemporary Western society.

VIENNA 1903

"The Modern Cult of Monuments" can be related to a specific set of problems with restoration in *fin-de-siècle* Vienna.[7] In 1903 Riegl had been appointed Conservator General at the *k. k. Zentral-Kommission für Erforschung und Erhaltung der Kunst-und historischen Denkmale*, (Central Commission for Artistic and Historical Monuments), reducing his teaching and research commitments as professor of art history at the University of Vienna.[8] He had earlier experience of the delicate problems of conservation. Before gaining his professorship he had worked for over a decade in the Museum of Applied

Art in Vienna as a curator at the textile department.[9] Notably Riegl's increasingly strong criticism of the museum's nationalist agenda, its aim of establishing an Austrian style through the support of and education in vernacular craft, had stalled his career in the museum.

Riegl's criticism of the museum's ambitions sheds interesting light on his theories on conservation.[10] Riegl saw the production of art as intimately connected to the economic and social system of a society. In a capitalist economy, vernacular art bound to a household economy was, he argued, doomed to extinction. The notion of exchange value was alien to the household economy, which produced these objects without the acknowledgement of a market. He argued therefore that vernacular art could not be protected by a system of support such as that initiated by the Museum of Applied Art, which foresaw its continued production as a commodity for an urban audience. Rather than continuing such policies, which merely disguised a bluntly capitalistic enterprise, the museum, Riegl argued, should take a more altruistic role. Instead of artificially maintaining a dying culture it should carefully collect and document the traces left before that culture was entirely lost. Saved as the past of the Austrian people the vernacular object would then gain an affective rather than a commercial value.[11]

Riegl's activities in the Commission for the Preservation of Monuments in Austria and his essay "The Modern Cult of Monuments" both bear the stamp of the underlying museological thoughts expressed in the criticism of the Museum of Applied Art. In dealing with the intricacies of governmental policy and everyday practicalities of conservation Riegl would attempt to formulate a theory of conservation that tried to transcend the limitations he perceived in the nationalist attitude of the museum.

Shortly before his appointment to the Central Commission Riegl engaged himself in an infected debate on the proper restoration of Vienna Cathedral.[12] The debate had emerged as a response to a restoration proposal by the architect Friedrich Schmidt, which suggested an extensive reconstruction of the cathedral's western portal. The group of artists that formed the Secessionist movement attacked the proposal, quoting John Ruskin's *Seven Lamps of Architecture* extensively to suggest that irreplaceable qualities would be destroyed if the restoration were carried out according to Schmidt's plan. Riegl intervened in the debate with an article "*Das Riesenthor zu St. Stephan*", 1902, in the *Neue Freie Presse* but took a diplomatic approach.[13] His article argued that both sides were equally modern in their opinions but that these emerged out of radically different desires. The side arguing for the reconstruction was directed by an art historical interest that wished to recover a lost coherence of style, while the side that rejected the reconstruction favoured the cathedral as an ageing assemblage of shifting styles that revealed the passage of time. Riegl pointed out that the different approaches were irreconcilable; reconstruction could not be combined with a sentiment for age itself.[14]

This type of conflict marked the discourse on conservation at the time not only in Vienna but in Europe as a whole. [15] The remarkable contribution of Riegl was that he tried not just to define but also to suggest a legal protection for this new *sentiment* for age; as noted the essay "The Modern Cult of Monuments" was written by Riegl as an introduction to a new law on conservation. [16]

With his essay and legal draft Riegl outlined how a new sentiment for age would define the monument for the twentieth century. To articulate a framework for guarding this sentiment was a task however that would prove both difficult and premature. The law was never fully accepted either during Riegl's time or later, and even though the "Venice Charter" of 1964 took up several aspects from the law proposal, Riegl's radical proposition that everything older than 60 years would fall under the category of the monument was not included. [17]

Even if Riegl's writing can be explained as a direct response to the conservation debate in Vienna, it is intriguing how visionary and complex the text remains. It goes beyond local politics to reflect at large on the phenomena of conservation. As an accompaniment to the law proposal, "The Modern Cult of Monuments" provides a fascinating insight into the difficulties that an attempt to base legislation on a 'feeling for age' must have experienced. After a few paragraphs Riegl loses sight of the inaugural objective of explaining the rationale of the law, and the text turns into a highly speculative meditation on the sociological and cultural effects of the cult of monuments. It is specifically in these speculative parts that Riegl's essay proves to be most productive in suggesting a novel reading of the role of the monument in modern society. These, rather than a contextualisation of Riegl's text as a whole, are the subject of the analysis made here.

THE MONUMENT

Riegl opens his essay with a definition of the monument that he directly parenthesises: "A monument", Riegl writes, "in its oldest and most original sense is a human creation, erected for a specific purpose of keeping single human deeds or events alive in the minds of future generations." [18] Riegl points out that the erection and care of such 'intentional' commemorative monuments still exists and can be traced back to the beginning of human culture. And yet, Riegl suggests, these monuments are no longer central: "when we talk about the modern cult and preservation of monuments, we are thinking not about 'intentional' monuments, but about monuments of art and history...." [19]

However, Riegl notes that even this definition of the monument is too reductive, for it does not acknowledge that the concept of an absolute inviolable canon of art has successively given way to a modern relative "art-value". [20] Riegl argues that classification into either art-monuments or historical-monuments gives rise to misunderstandings and suggests instead a classification of 'intentional' and 'unintentional' monuments.

"Everything that has been and is no longer we call historical."[21] Riegl saw the development of heritage as a phenomenon closely connected to a modern perception of history caught in the knowledge that what has been can never be again. In this notion of the irreplaceability of every event, of the mortality of culture itself, modern man submits to artefacts left from a time that has passed. These cult objects consisted largely of what Riegl termed unintentional monuments. Unintentional in so far as they where not erected with the purpose of commemorating any specific event or person but still monuments in their irreplaceable value for modern man.

With his concept of the unintentional monument Riegl makes a brutal expansion in the definition of a monument to incorporate in the end every artefact without regard to its original significance and purpose as long as it reveals the passage of a considerable period of time.[22] Age becomes the sign that defines the object as a monument.

AGE

It is necessary to complicate the notion of age in order to grasp the shift from the cult of the intentional monument to the cult of the unintentional, which Riegl argues characterises Western history from the period of the Renaissance. Age is a complex concept; it talks both of identification and distance. An intentional monument, erected to commemorate a human deed or event, always has the purpose of overcoming distance, to in one sense refuse the passage of time. With its physical presence it aims to create a lapse in time that renders the past present and establishes a transparent connection to the event or the person that the monument is to commemorate. The intentional monument's primary function according to Riegl, is to maintain memory alive; to arrest, one might say, the soft forgetfulness of history. For the intentional monument, therefore, age is always an obstacle. Indeed the intentional monument is dependent on a non-aged appearance to maintain its function as a memorial; any signs of decay would suggest a diminishing interest in the subject whose presence in memory it governs. The tradition of erecting monuments in durable materials follows this logic: hard polished surfaces reject the signs of age and those personal identifications that always threaten the rhetoric of the monument by diverting it away from its vocation, to the intimate history of its beholders. This is why the temptation to scribble over monuments is often felt so urgently, a need to break the inert stasis of the monument and bring in a temporal dimension of life.

Riegl's concept of the unintentional monument on the other hand suggests a radically different logic in which the enigma of absence is central. Where intentional monuments in some sense always suppress loss through the articulation of triumph or martyrdom, these unintentional monuments leave loss at the centre. Not purposely built as monuments, they are found in the inflated realm of heritage as 'historical objects' that reject a transparent presence in preference for an obscured and distant past.

Riegl underlines that both the intentional and the unintentional monument are characterised by a commemorative value. Crucially, however, while the value of the intentional monument is always conditioned by its makers—the monument is cared for as long as the person or event it is to commemorate is still remembered—the value of the unintentional monument is relative and, as Riegl points out, left to us to define: "when we call such works of art 'monuments' it is a subjective rather than an objective designation" Riegl notes, continuing further: "we have defined the value of the unintentional ones".[23] This is a crucial observation and points to an important distinction between the intentional and the unintentional monument. While the intentional monument, purposely erected to commemorate, appears as a trans-historical, almost ubiquitous phenomenal, the unintentional monument is a datable invention of the West whose history and origin Riegl traces back to the Italian Renaissance.[24] Riegl's historical account of the 'invention' of the unintentional monument can be questioned; he does not, for example, pay any attention to the impact of the French Revolution in the conception of the unintentional monument as a defined category. But his clear identification of the unintentional monument is, I would argue, crucial to understanding the phenomena of heritage; particularly its explosive development and expansion in Western society.

CONSERVATION

Riegl noted that *we* define the value of the unintentional monument. In his highly visually orientated analysis, the onlooker constructed the monument. Riegl abandoned the classification of the monuments themselves to instead identify and distinguish between values applied to them, and these values were almost exclusively based on the visual effect of the monument upon the beholder.

After his summary of the evolution in history from the cult of the intentional monument to the modern cult of unintentional monuments, Riegl continues his essay by classifying and identifying the different values attributed to the monument, and speculates how these values determined the conservation of the monument. Should the monument be reconstructed to regain its completeness and coherence of form or should it be allowed to disintegrate, to return to nature? Riegl's answer to this question is that this depends on which value the monument in question has for the beholder. However, as Riegl shows, these values often conflict and demand different kinds of conservation strategies for the same object.

Riegl distinguishes three forms of memory-values (*Erinnerungswerte*) that effect the care of the monument: intentional commemorative-value (*gewollter Erinnerungswert*), historical-value (*historischer Wert*) and age-value (*Alterswert*). The first, intentional commemorative-value relates only to the class of intentional monuments; the two last, historical-value and age-value, relate to the class of unintentional monuments and are

THE MODERN CULT OF MONUMENTS

therefore part of the 'modern cult of monuments'. As the scope of memory-value widens, the different classes of monuments become contained within each other. The class of intentional monuments included only those works that recalled a specific moment from the past. The monuments to which a historical-value is designated still refer to a specific moment in history but they are unintentional in that the choice of monuments is left to our subjective preference. A monument that was originally 'just' an intentional monument can therefore be incorporated into this class if it is defined as being of historical worth. The class of monuments relating to age-value is even more expansive in its scope. As was noted earlier Riegl's radical suggestion was that any artefact without regard to its original significance and purpose could gain an age-value that defined it as a monument as long as it revealed to the onlooker that a considerable period of time had passed since it was new.[25]

The three forms of memory-values, the *Erinnerungswerte*, Riegl identified all suggested different strategies of restoration. To maintain an intentional commemorative-value in the monument it had to be kept in a pristine state. Historical-value impinged on the monument defining a precise and authentic moment in history. The task of restoration when a historical-value was identified was to reconstruct the building back to its "original" state. This however always risked jeopardising the validity of the monument as a historical document. To prove what was original and what was not became an increasingly complex issue. Indeed in historical-value the document and the monument had become one and the same, and this contributed to the intricacy of conservation.[26]

To possess an age-value it was required that the monument display 'truthfully' the changes and evolutions it had undergone since its construction, communicating primarily the passage of time. Here restoration in itself was fundamentally problematic and was reduced to preventative measures to protect the objects from the corrosive forces of nature, modernisation or in contemporary times from the effects of the commercialisation of the object itself.

HISTORY

Riegl related the commemorative-values to the evolution of history. He suggested that his classes of monument form three consecutive phases of what the monument had meant, and that these phases could be traced in the history of conservation. In his schema the development evolves from the cult of the intentional monument to the recognition of a historical value in the monument. Riegl argued, in a lightly disguised criticism of pedantic art historical scholarship, that through the evolution of refined scholarship even the smallest particularity in the developmental chain began to be recognised as irreplaceable. This notion of the irreplacebility of every event would lead to the notion of developmental value in which the particulars were ultimately unimportant. The value of the monument would reside no longer in its historicity, its specific relation to a historical period, but in its capacity for revealing the process of development itself, the cycle of death and life. This appreciation of the process of evolution, of the passage of time, Riegl termed age-value. This value was the result of the recognition of historical-value but in the end it would challenge and replace it.

The shift from historical value to age-value destabilises the notion of the national monument that so closely underwrote the nineteenth century's discourse on conservation. The narrative core of the national monument was an identification with a people: the race, the 'folk' that with their hands had transformed matter into buildings. This characteristic definition can be seen in the theories of Eugène-Emmanuel Violett-le-Duc and John Ruskin. In Riegl's age-value, on the other hand, the issue of identification lies between the viewing subject, the observer in the here and now, and the building itself:

> In the twentieth century we appreciate particularly the purely natural cycle of becoming and passing away.... Thus modern man sees a bit of himself in a monument, and he will react to every intervention as he would to one on himself.[27]

Riegl's notion of age-value radicalised the notion of the monument as narrative. Where Viollet-le-Duc and Ruskin, despite their contrasting ideas, both position the monument as a historical document (of momentary origin or of continuous action); in Riegl, art history is replaced with a corporal identification that suggests an altogether different relation between man and objects. While nineteenth century restorations were carried out under the aegis of completing or preserving the archive of buildings that together formed a national inventory and history of architecture, Riegl's monument appears as a melancholic object, revealing the constant ruination of the archive *per se*.

According to Riegl's prophecy, age-value was the most modern value and the one that would guide the conservation of the monument in the future.[28] However Riegl emphasised that the all-embracing value of age had yet to come, and that the contemporary conflict in conservation was often played out between historical-value and age-value. Through his careful classification and naming of different values he shows not only how different memory-values conflict and demand different strategies of conservation, but also how the memory-values themselves are often antithetical to what Riegl named present-day-values (*Gegenwartswerte*).

THE PRESENT

Riegl acknowledged that the monument fulfilled other purposes relating not to commemoration but to use and aesthetic enjoyment. He noted that these present-day-values were strictly speaking not part of the modern cult of monuments, as they denied the memorial function of the monument; and yet they effected the conservation of the monument nonetheless, and were therefore crucial to identify. He classified these present-day-values into two main groups: use-value and art-value. The first group referred to the practical functional performance of the object, the second to its aesthetic value for the beholder. The use-value of a monument tends to stand in conflict with the monument's commemorative-value, both the historical- but especially the more modern age-value.[29] While age-value emerges out of gradual dissolution, the dissolving of form and colour revealing the passage of time, use-value requires the maintenance of the object—the conflict is evident.

Riegl's notion of art-value is more complex and is closely related to his concept of *Kunstwollen*, the idea of a relative and changing notion of art specific to every period and culture in history. Riegl's untranslatable and controversial concept was central not only to his view on the function of art in society but also to his theory of art history, its scope and limitations. The practices, aesthetics and concepts of a given culture and period generated a shared intention, drive or urge—*Kunstwollen*—which guided artistic production; a close formal interpretation of these works of art revealed the world-view of the society in which they were created. Emphasising the specificity of every period and culture, Riegl's *Kunstwollen* is an explicit rejection of any universal values in art and also crucially of the notion of progress and decline in the evolution of art that dominated the art historical tradition of the time. As every period or culture created art according to its *Kunstwollen*, its need of art, it was irrelevant to perceive one period or culture as inferior to another. Riegl's art-value was then relative and changing as well as specific to every period and culture in history.[30]

To possess art-value Riegl claimed, it was required that the object was a discrete entity, which revealed no decay in shape or colour.[31] In Riegl's schema art-value did not, then, necessarily conflict with historical-value, even if these values were generated from different positions—the first in relation to present-day-value, the other from the commemorative-value of the monument. The identification of a historical value in the monument had often resulted in the reconstruction of the object as new, and in its completeness and integrity it could therefore satisfy an art-value.

Age-value on the other hand conflicted strongly with art-value. It was the very ageing, the process of dissolution into the general that generated age-value and anything, independent of any previous aesthetic properties, could gain it. Indeed, a monument that was appreciated for its age-value was nothing more than a catalyst which triggered in the beholder a sense of the life cycle. Age-value was not, then, bound up with the object. As Riegl dramatically expressed it: "the object has shrunk to a necessary evil".[32] Indeed independently of either the historical or the aesthetic quality that had originally defined the unintentional monument, age-value would fundamentally question the notion of the monument altogether. Art-value on the other hand was closely bound to the object. To satisfy both art-value and age-value in the same object was therefore unfeasible:

... where the monument's conception, shape, and colour satisfy our modern *Kunstwollen*, it follows that this value should not be allowed to diminish in significance in order to conform to the expectations of age-value.[33]

The strongest opposition to age-value, however is what Riegl terms newness-value (*Neuheitswert*). For Riegl the aesthetic of the new was always involved with completeness: while signs of age appeal to modern man, signs of decay on the new are generally disturbing. It was the completeness of the new, Riegl claimed, which distinguished modernity itself from the past: "In our modern view, the new artefact requires flawless integrity of form and colour as well as style; that is to say, the truly modern work must, in its concept and detail, recall earlier work as little as possible." [34] With truly modernistic ambition Riegl wanted to break with the historicism of the nineteenth century. He rejected the thought that the new could emerge from art historical studies.[35] The new, he argued, had to gain its quality specifically by differentiating itself from the old.

The dichotomy between age-value and newness-value emerges in the next chapter in relation to Le Corbusier's modernisation of Paris. What should be noted here is that Riegl intriguingly and acutely places newness-value as a class belonging to art-value. Riegl's radical proposition therefore is that the new always has an art-value. Riegl designated the new a specific power in modern society that can be compared with that he designated to the aged. In its integrity and purity the new could be appreciated by anyone. No education was needed to appreciate its smooth and even surfaces, he argued, anticipating Sigfried Giedion's argument about streamlining in *Mechanization Takes Command*, 1948.[36]

Spatially distinct—the new clearly confined within its borders, the old disintegrating into its surroundings—these two opposites in Riegl's schema would both in their visual directness become a force in a mass-society. The dichotomy between the attraction of the shiny new and the feeling for the aged would compete in a world of objects. Riegl, writing on the brim of modernism, predicted that the attraction of the new was stronger than that of the old. The masses' love for the new, Riegl saw as the largest hindrance to a general recognition of age-value: "The masses have always enjoyed new things.... What is rooted in thousands of years of perception—namely the priority of youth over age—cannot be eliminated in a few decades."[37] A century later the situation appears somewhat qualified. The comfort of the old and familiar dominates popular discourse, specifically perhaps in the realm of housing and urbanism whose rhetoric nearly without exception looks backwards. Riegl's prophecy that the force of the old would conquer the masses seems to have been fulfilled to an extent that he could hardly have foreseen.

Riegl, however, saw the power of age as a potential for the new; the cult of the old would free the new from its historical burden. As we have seen Riegl's age-value placed the monument firmly in the realm of the old were it was isolated from the functionality and use of the everyday. The old was not to be directly reused but only to return to the present in the form of its otherness, as the *cult* of the old. The new on the other hand defined its newness by its very coherence with the present, its oneness with the time. A paradoxical theme emerges: the valuation of ancient monuments in the modern era depends on a clear distinction between the old and the new. The concern of restoration is to establish and maintain this difference; indeed restoration becomes in some sense the apparatus used to define the modern itself.

THE CULT

Riegl had entitled his essay the modern *cult* of monuments.[40] Under Riegl's dry prose one can find a belief that heritage in a secular society will fill the void left by religion. The cult of heritage would turn into a mass-movement that ignored borders and national identities; in the face of age all monuments were equal. Organised around a sentiment for age Riegl envisioned heritage as a supranational cult that, like Christianity, would reach out to the masses:

> ... age-value conveys the achievements of scholarship to everyone, as it spends in emotion what intellect has fashioned. This is comparable to what Christianity provided for the masses in late antiquity.... Considered in the light of human reason rather than divine revelation, the masses could not be won with logical argumentation, but only by a direct appeal to their emotions and needs.[41]

Riegl underlined that modern man needed the old: "An era seeking aesthetic redemption through the art cannot do without monuments of earlier periods", he wrote.[42] This need for the old jarred with Riegl's concept of *Kunstwollen*. The 'urge' or 'will' to art specific to every historic period and context suggested that only new works could be appreciated fully by a modern beholder; only the new was in tune with the present notion of art. And yet modern man valued the old:

> It seems natural for old monuments not to possess art-value for later generations, especially when they belong to the remote past; but we know from experience that works of art created centuries ago can frequently be valued much more than modern ones.[43]

Certain works from the past transcended their historical contexts and addressed the modern viewer despite their remoteness and age. And yet this meeting with work from past times could never be the same as the confrontation with a new work. The space of time was always there. This distance, between a now and a then, turned the meeting into a special one:

> It is precisely this apparent correspondence of the modern *Kunstwollen* and certain aspects of historical art which, in its conflicting nature, exerts such power over the modern viewer.[44]

In a spiral of ambiguity certain objects of the past appeared to be at one with the present *Kunstwollen* and yet the signs of age, manifested in patina or in estranged and outmoded forms, removed them from the present to a distant past. I should suggest that it is this subtle interplay between the apparent accessibility and the simultaneous non-existence of the past that generates the longing, or to use Riegl's term the 'cult' of the past, in secularised society. The old object suggests the possibility of a reunion and yet withdraws into its pastness. This double play between proximity and distance evokes the desire for the old in modern society.

THE PAST AS UTOPIA

Riegl's essay "The Modern Cult of Monuments" shows the task of conservation in its full complexity. The essay goes beyond the debate on how monuments should be restored to the very question of *why* we care for monuments in Western culture. For Riegl different strategies of conservation revealed the world-view of a specific period; the value of the monument was key to a larger interrogation of a society and its condition. Riegl's focus on the cult of the monument rather than on the monuments themselves, makes his essay still stand out as an unprecedented and deeply original contribution to the study of the phenomena of conservation and the role of its objects in a secularised and capitalist society.

Inevitably, some aspects of Riegl's analysis appear bounded by his time and context. His identification of three memory-values based on intention, history and age suggest a historical determinism imbued with a utopian desire. Riegl invested the cult of the old with altruistic dimensions that would supersede the egoistic desires of the individual and the nation. In his schema the historical process evolved from the cult of the intentional monument, to the desire to preserve the monument for its historical significance to a given culture—the nationalistic monument—to reach finally the stage of a cult of the universal value of age. This final stage on the evolution of the cult of monuments would go across national and social stratification. Age, Riegl argued, was a ubiquitous phenomenon that knew no borders; its expression was accessible to all. Age, then, appeared as a value that challenged the contextualism of *Kunstwollen*. Where Riegl's notion of art being specific to every period and culture rejected the idea of universal values, his notion of age-value identified an effect that was universal. Writing near the end of the Austrian Empire, in a political climate marked by the rising demand of ethnic minorities for self-determination and an increasing xenophobia feeding on the myth of nationalism, Riegl remarkably put forward a notion of the monument that rejected national narrative in favour of the homogenising cross- cultural qualities and effects of age.[45]

Riegl's prediction that the cult of intentional monuments, as a trace of an archaic tradition, would not survive a modern notion of history was to be proved wrong. As noted at the start of this chapter, the World Wars and totalitarian regimes of the twentieth century were both to lead to the re-affirmation of the role the intentional monument and to the use of the historical monument in the fabrication of national myths. Generally, Riegl's historical determinism is now of historical rather than analytical interest. The fall of the Soviet Union would show how fast intentional monuments can move over to the category of the unintentional; after the initial overthrow and fragmentation of the monuments identified with the power machines of totalitarian states, they quickly became collectible items and tokens for sentimental reverie over 'bad' old times. The historicisation and aestheticisation of these former intentional monuments suggests in contradistinction to Riegl, that the notion of the monument does not follow a given evolution. Rather, as this book has argued as one of its main points, the notion of the monument finds its historic specificity in different political and spatial regimes.

Riegl's "Modern Cult of Monuments" does contain a valuable legacy, however. His identification of the unintentional monument as a class remains a fruitful category for analytical thinking and has informed this book's analysis of the phenomenon of conservation. While Riegl's historical context prevented him from seeing the euro-centric perspective of his historical schema, his history of conservation clearly shows how the emergence of the unintentional monument is specific to Western culture.

The internal contradictions that shift through "The Modern Cult of Monuments" also reveal intriguing complexities that contribute to widen the notion of the monument. Both in his essay and in his law-proposal Riegl had defined the monument as "a human creation, erected for a specific purpose of keeping single human deeds or events alive in the minds of future generations". Throughout his examination of the notion of the monument and its function in the age of modernity Riegl maintained that the monument's primary function was to provoke memories (*Erinnerungen*). However, Riegl's notion of the unintentional monument and his identification of modern age-value suggest at the same time that the memory function of the monument, as well as the very monument itself, will in the end be made redundant. With age-value the monument is reduced to matter that exposes the process of aging in its disintegration. The intentional monument's logic of duration, expressed in its hard and durable surfaces, had governed the memory of its commissioner. Riegl's record of the history of conservation revealed on the other hand how the monument has gradually been transformed from an object that originally communicated permanence to an object that was about fragility and loss, removed from the present for reasons of history and sentiment.

BIBLIOGRAPHICAL SUMMARY

A shorter version of this chapter has been published as "The Cult of Age in Mass Society: Alois Riegl's theory of conservation", *Future Anterior, Journal of Historic Preservation, History Theory and Criticism*, Vol. 1, No. 1, spring 2004, pp. 74–80 and as "The Fragile Monument: On Alois Riegl's Modern Cult of Monuments" in *(theorising) History in architecture and design*, Elisabeth Tostrup and Cristian Hermanssen eds., Oslo: AHO, 2003, pp. 33–39.

As an introduction to the historical background to formalist art history Michael Podro's two books, *The Manifolds in Perception and The Critical Historians of Art* benefitted this chapter (Podro, Michael, *The Manifolds in Perception: Theories of Art from Kant to Hildebrand*, Oxford: Clarendon Press, 1972 and *The Critical Historians of Art*, New Haven and London: Yale University Press, 1982.) Helpful also were the translations of several central texts in this tradition that appeared in the publication *Empathy, Form and Space; Problems in German Aesthetics 1873–1893*, Harry F Mallgrave ed., Santa Monica: Getty Center, 1994. Mark Jarzombek's revealing article "De-Scribing the Language of Looking; Wölfflin and the History of Aesthetic Experientialism" was crucial for my understanding of the impact of formalist theory on post-war architectural history and theory (Jarzombek, Mark, "De-Scribing the Language of Looking; Wölfflin and the History of Aesthetic Experientialism", *Assemblage* 23, 1994, pp. 28–69).

Comparably few studies of Riegl's scholarship exist and until recently relatively few of Riegl's writing had been translated into English. This can partly be explained by Riegl's heavy-handed prose but crucially also by the in part very unhappy appropriation of his research theory by the so-called *Vienna School*. The school coalesced around two scholars, Otto Pächt, a Jew, who was forced to leave Austria in 1938, and Hans Sedlmayr, who later became an outspoken supporter of National Socialism. Inspired by Riegl's research method Pächt and Sedlmayr founded in the 30s the short-lived journal, *Kunstwissenschaftliche Forschungen*, used as platform for their idea for a new method of 'rigorous' art history. Although the first volume was favourably reviewed by Walter Benjamin (Benjamin, Walter, "Rigorous Study of Art" (1931/1933), Thomas Y Levin trans., *October*, 47, 1988, pp. 84–90, see also Levin, Thomas, Y, "Benjamin and the Theory of Art History. An Introduction to the 'Rigorous Study of Art'", *October*, 47, 1988, pp. 77–83), Sedlmayr's extreme conservatism quickly coloured his scholarship and his political affiliations came to overshadow the work of the *Vienna School* as whole.

The history of the *Vienna School*'s political development has tainted the reception of Riegl, specifically in the English context. The influential art historian Ernst Gombrich, a younger contemporary of Sedlmayr in Vienna, who as Pächt was forced to flee to England, opens his *Art and Illusion* from 1960 with an attack on Riegl. Gombrich, influenced by the philosopher Karl Popper' critique of historicism, saw in Riegl's scholarship a totalitarian tendency and linked Riegl's concept of *Kunstwollen* to the inherent problems of concepts such as race, mankind and ages (Gombrich, Ernst, *Art and Illusion: a Study in Psychology of Pictorial Representation*, Princeton, New Jersey: Princeton University Press, 1960).

More recent Anglo-Saxon scholarship has tried to go beyond Gombrich's judgement of Riegl. Michel Podro's study of the foundation of art history as a discipline was a first reassessment of Riegl's work, (Podro, Michael, *The Critical Historians of Art*, New Haven and London: Yale University Press, 1982). Before that, Pächt in an article in the *Burlington Magazine* discussed Riegl's scholarship in positive terms (Pächt, Otto, "Art Historians and Art Critics—VI: Alois Riegl", *Burlington Magazine*, 105, 1963, pp. 188–193) and in 1979 Henri Zerner in the American journal *Daedalus* moderated Gombrich's critique of Riegl's historicism (Zerner, Henri, "Alois Riegl: Art, Value, and Historicism", *Daedalus*, 105 (1976), pp. 177–178).

The strong focus in later years on Walter Benjamin, who was strongly influenced by Riegl, has renewed the interest in Riegl's scholarship within art history and translations of central texts are appearing. Two readers reflect this new interest in Riegl, *The Vienna School Reader and Framing Formalism* (Wood, Christopher, S, ed., *The Vienna School Reader: Politics and Art Historical Method in the 1930s*, New York: Zone Books, 2000, and *Framing Formalism: Riegl's Work*, Richard Woodfield, ed., Amsterdam: G+B Arts International, 2001).

The beginning of the 90s saw the first two full length studies of Riegl's scholarship in English: Margaret Olin's *Forms of Representation in Alois Riegl's Theory of Art*, Pennsylvania: Pennsylvania University Press, 1992 and Margaret Iversen's *Alois Riegl: Art History and Theory*, Cambridge, MA, and London: MIT Press, 1993. With their different orientation, the first acknowledging Mikhail Bakhtin's interest in Riegl and Riegl's contribution to formal artistic discourse, the latter emphasising Riegl's method of interpretation, both studies have been important for this chapter. In 2006 Michael Gubser's *Time's visible surface : Alois Riegl and the discourse on history and temporality in Fin-de-siècle Vienna*, was published, which takes up similar problematics to those considered in this chapter. Gubser Michael, *Time's visible surface: Alois Riegl and the discourse on history and temporality in Fin-de-siècle Vienna*, Detroit: Wayne State University Press, 2006 . The as yet unpublished study by Diana Graham Reynolds, which considers in detail Riegl's institutional and political context, has also been most valuable for developing my argument for this chapter (Reynolds, Diana Graham, "Alois Riegl and the Politics of Art History: Intellectual Traditions and Austrian Identity in *Fin-de-Siècle* Vienna", PhD Dissertation, San Diego: University of California/Ann Arbor: (UMI) 1997).

If the interest in Riegl's art historical writing has been somewhat hesitant to develop, the opposite is true of his writing in the field of conservation. The essay "Der moderne Denkmalkultus. Sein Wesen und seine Entstehung", from 1903 was the first text of Riegl that was translated in its entirety into English. The American architectural journal *Oppositions* provided a translation of the essay in 1982, and the issue also included a lengthy analysis of the text by the architectural historian Kurt W Foster that has been useful for this chapter (Riegl, Alois, "The Modern Cult of Monuments: Its Character and Its Origin", pp. 21–51 and Forster, Kurt W, "Monument/Memory and the Mortality of Architecture", both in *Oppositions*, 25, Fall, 1982, pp. 2–18). A French translation appeared in 1984 with a preface by Françoise Choay who, like Forster argued for the current relevance of the essay (Riegl, Alois, *Le Culte moderne des monuments, Son essence et sa genèse*, Paris: Seuil, 1984). In a wider conservation context a shortened version of the essay appeared in English translation in the Getty Foundation Readings in Conservation in 1996 (*Historical and Philosophical Issues in the Conservation of Cultural Heritage*, Getty Foundation, Los Angeles, 1996) and the essay was also reprinted in *Konservieren, nicht restaurieren. Streitschriften zur Denkmalpflege um 1900* in 1988, (Bauwelt Fundamente, Friedr. Vieweg & Sohn, Braunschweig, 1988), and again in 1995 in *Kunstwerk oder Denkmal? Alois Riegls Schriften zur Denkmalpflege*, Ernst Bacher ed., Wien, Köln and Weimar: Böhlau Verlag, 1995. In 1995 the essay was translated into Italian and published in an anthology that also included a compilation of several scholarly comments on Riegl's essay, *Alois Riegl: teoria e prassi della conservazione dei monumenti*, Sandro Scarrocchia, ed., Bologna: Cooperativa Libraria Universitaria Editrice Bologna, 1995. The essay has also been translated in part into Norwegian (*Agora: journal for metafysisk spekulasjon*, Oslo, 2006, pp. 203–216).

Through these various re-editions and translations Riegl's thoughts and arguments about conservation have become accessible to a wide range of scholars and this chapter has been written partly as a response to such comments and interpretations of "The Modern Cult of Monuments". Margaret Olin's article "The Cult of Monuments as a State Religion in late 19th Century Austria" has been central to my analysis in that Olin is one of the few scholars writing on the essay who have tried to problematise Riegl's notion of the monument (Olin, Margaret, "The Cult of Monuments as a State Religion in late nineteenth Century Austria", *Wiener Jahrbuch für Kunstgeschichte*, 38, 1985, pp. 177–198). Otherwise, specifically within the field of conservation, scholars mostly praise Riegl for his careful identification of different values in conservation. In a Scandinavian context Dag Myklebust has lifted forward Riegl contribution and Göran Kåring writing in 1992 calls Riegl's analysis ground-breaking and has traced the impact of Riegl's thoughts in Austrian and German policies of conservation (Myklebust, Dag, "Verditenkning—en arbeidsmåte i bygningsvern", *Fortidsminneforeningens årbok*, 1981, pp. 85–106, and Kåring, Göran, *När medeltidens sol gått ned*, Stockholm: Kungl. Vitterhets Historie och Antikvitets Akademien, 1992). Françoise Choay in her *L'allégorie du patrimoine*, also from 1992, sees Riegl as the synthesis between the conflicting theories of Viollet-le-Duc and Ruskin, and emphasises that Riegl was the first to clearly identify the historical monument as a separate category (Choay, Françoise, *L'allégorie du patrimoine*, Paris: Seuil, 1992). Ernst Batchen writing in 1995 underlined that Riegl's essay is the first systematic analysis of heritage values, a point argued also by Scarrocchia referred to above. In Jukka Jokilehto's overview of conservation history (Jokilehto, Jukka, *A History of Architectural Conservation*, Oxford: Butterworth-Heinemann, 1999), Riegl's arguments are carefully summarised and their impact acknowledged.

I am thankful to Inken Witt for valuable comments on the English translation of "The Modern Cult of Monument", both in conversation and in her MA thesis (Witt, Inken, "Der moderne Denkmalkultus. Sein Wesen und seine Entstehung", MA dissertation, Architectural Association, London, 1997).

PRIMARY SOURCES

Riegl, Alois:

The Group Portraiture of Holland (Das holländische Gruppenporträt, Jahrbuch des allerhöchsten Kaiserhauses 23, 1902), Evelyn M Kain and David Britt trans., introduction Wolfgang Kemp, Los Angeles: Getty Research Institute for the History of Art and the Humanities, 1999.

Problems of Style: Foundations for a History of Ornament (*Stilfragen*, Siemens, Berlin 1893), Evelyn Kain trans., annotations and introduction by David Castriota, preface by Henrik Zerner, Princeton and New York: Princeton University Press, 1992.

Late Roman Art Industry, (*Die spätrömische Kunstindustrie nach den Funden in Österreich-Ungarn*, Vienna: I Teil, K k Hof-und Staatsdruckerei, 1901), Rolf Winkes trans., Rome Bretschneider, 1985.

The origins of Baroque art in Rome (Entstehung der Barockkunst in Rom, Vienna 1908), Andrew Hopkins and Arnold Witte eds. and trans., with essays by Alina Payne, Arnold Witte, and Andrew Hopkins, Los Angeles: Getty Research Institute, 2010.

"The Modern Cult of Monuments: Its Character and Its Origin", ("Der moderne Denkmalkultus. Sein Wesen und seine Entstehung", Vienna, 1903, republished in *Konservieren, nicht restaurieren. Streitschriften zur Denkmalpflege um 1900*, Braunschweig: Bauwelt Fundamente, Friedr. Vieweg & Sohn, 1988), trans. Kurt Forster and Diane Ghirardo, in *Oppositions*, 25, 1982, pp. 21–51. French translation: *Le Culte moderne des monuments, Son essence et sa genèse*, Daniel Wieczorek trans., Paris: Seuil, 1984. Hereafter referred to as "The Modern Cult of Monuments". References in this chapter are to the Forster and Ghirardo edition unless otherwise noted.

NOTES

[1] Riegl, Alois, "The Modern Cult of Monuments: Its Character and Its Origin", ("Der moderne Denkmalkultus. Sein Wesen und seine Entstehung", Vienna, 1903, republished in *Konservieren, nicht restaurieren. Streitschriften zur Denkmalpflege um 1900*, Braunschweig: Bauwelt Fundamente, Friedr. Vieweg & Sohn, 1988), trans. Kurt Forster and Diane Ghirardo, in *Oppositions*, 25, 1982, pp. 21–51. French translation: *Le Culte moderne des monuments, Son essence et sa genèse*, transl. D, Wieczorek, Paris: Seuil, 1984. Hereafter referred to as "The Modern Cult of Monuments". References in this chapter are to the Forster/Girardo edition unless otherwise noted.

[2] The term "space" has of course itself a history, from Kant's *Critique of Pure Reason*, 1781, where space existed in the mind *a priori*, to Hegel's *Lectures on Aesthetics* and Gottfried Semper's *Der Stil*, that in different ways argued the primacy of enclosure over material; from Robert Vischer's theory of empathy predicated on the notion of bodily sensations in space, developed in *On the Optical Sense of Form*, 1873, to the speculative essays of Adolf Hildebrand (*The Problems of Form in the Fine Arts*, 1893) and August Schmarsow (*The Essence of Architectural Creation*, 1893), who both in different ways started to describe space as a continuum that could give form to architecture rather than the other way around. Riegl's use of the term actively developed its content. His *Late Roman Art-Industry*, 1901, imagined the perception of space as going through different evolutionary steps, from a form of haptic-objective perception that visualised objects in space, to an optic-subjective perception in which the object and the surroundings merge in an optical unity. See: Kant, Immanuel, *The Critique of Pure Reason* (1781), N Kemp Smith trans., London: Macmillan, 1929; Hegel, Georg Wilhelm Friedrich, *Aesthetics*, TM Knox trans., Oxford: Oxford University Press, 2 Vols., 1975; Gottfried Semper, *Der Stil in den technischen und tectonischen Künsten oder praktische Aesthetik*, Frankfurt: 2 Vols., 1860, 1863 (part of *Der Stil* is translated in *The Four Elements of Architecture and Other Writings*, Harry Mallgrave trans., Cambridge: Cambridge University Press, 1989); Riegl, Alois, *Late Roman Art Industry*, (*Die spätrömische Kunstindustrie nach den Funden in Österreich-Ungarn*, Vienna: I Teil, K k Hof-und Staatsdruckerei, 1901), Rolf Winkes trans., Rome: Bretschneider, 1985. The essays of Robert Vischer, "On the Optical Sense of Form: a contribution to Aesthetics"; Adolf Hildebrand, "The Problems of Form in the Fine Arts"; and August Schamarsow, "The Essence of Architectural Creation" are all translated and published in *Empathy, Form and Space; Problems in German Aesthetics 1873–1893*, Harry F Mallgrave ed., Santa Monica: Getty Center , 1994.

3 Riegl, Alois, *Problems of Style: Foundations for a History of Ornament* (*Stilfragen*, Siemens, Berlin 1893) transl. Evelyn Kain, annotations and introduction by David Castriota, preface by Henrik Zerner, Princeton and New York: Princeton University Press, 1992. Riegl, Alois, *Late Roman Art Industry*, (*Die spätrömische Kunstindustrie nach den Funden in Österreich-Ungarn*, I Teil, K k Hof-und Staatsdruckerei, Vienna 1901) trans. Rolf Winkes, Rome: Bretschneider, 1985 (conclusion also reprinted in Wood, Christopher, S, ed., *The Vienna School Reader, Politics and Art Historical Method in the 1930s*, New York: Zone Books, 2000 pp. 87–98). Riegl, Alois, *The Group Portraiture of Holland*, (Das holländische Gruppenporträt, Jahrbuch des allerhöchsten Kaiserhauses 23, 1902, pp. 71–278) transl. Evelyn M Kain and David Britt, with introduction by Wolfgang Kemp, Getty Research Institute for the History of Art and the Humanities, Los Angeles, California, 1999. Significant studies in art theory that consider the essay include Margaret Iversen's *Alois Riegl: Art History and Theory*, MIT Press, Cambridge, MA, and London, 1993; Margaret Olin's article, "The Cult of Monuments as a State Religion in late 19th Century Austria", *Wiener Jahrbuch für Kunstgeschichte*, 38, 1985, pp. 177–198 and her book *Forms of Representation in Alois Riegl's Theory of Art*, University Park, Pennsylvania: Pennsylvania State University Press, 1992.

4 For the reception of the essay in the field of conservation, see the bibliographical summary in this chapter.

5 In his essay "Monument and Memory in a Postmodern Age" Andreas Huyssen discusses with intellectual sharpness the controversial and problematic role of memory in contemporary society in relation to the Holocaust memorial, Huyssen, Andreas, "Monument and Memory in a Postmodern Age", *Yale Journal of Criticism*, 6, No. 2, 1993. See also Young, James E, *The Texture of Memory: Holocaust Memorials and Meaning*, New Haven and London: Yale University Press, 1993. Both Huyssen and Young have focused their analyses of memory and Holocaust on the issue of the Holocaust memorial. For a discussion of trauma and memory at an urban level, see Mark Jarzombek, Mark, *Urban Heterology, Dresden and the Dialectics of Post-traumatic History*, School of Architecture, Lund: Lund University, 2001.

6 Riegl, Alois, "The Modern Cult of Monuments", p. 34.

7 Margaret Olin has emphasised this contextual aspect of Riegl's essay: Olin, Margaret, "The Cult of Monuments as a State Religion in late 19th Century Austria", *Wiener Jahrbuch für Kunstgeschichte*, 38, 1985, pp. 177–198.

8 At the commission Riegl was the first to have a salaried position; previously the post of Conservator General (Director of the Commission) was an honorary one and Riegl's salaried post can be seen as an example of the increasing professionalisation of conservation as a discipline that took place in Europe at the turn of the century. See further Olin, Margaret, "The Cult of Monuments as a State Religion in late 19th Century Austria", *Wiener Jahrbuch für Kunstgeschichte*, 38, 1985, pp. 177–198., and Bacher, Ernst, *Kunstwerk oder Denkmal? Alois Riegls Schriften zur Denkmalpflege*, Wien, Köln and Weimar: Böhlau Verlag, 1995, pp. 13–19.

9 For a short biography of Alois Riegl see Pächt, Otto, "Art Historians and Art Critics" VI: Alois Riegl, *Burlington Magazine*, 105, 1963, pp. 188–193.

10 Diana Reynolds' study of Riegl's intellectual and institutional context, *Alois Riegl and the Politics of Art History*, is useful for understanding the complexity of this relationship. see Reynolds, Diana Graham, "Alois Riegl and the Politics of Art History: Intellectual Traditions and Austrian Identity in *Fin-de-Siècle* Vienna", PhD Dissertation, University of California at San Diego, 1997/Ann Arbor: (UMI) 1997, Chapter 5 (pp. 129–180)

11 Reynolds, Diana Graham, "Alois Riegl and the Politics of Art History: Intellectual Traditions and Austrian Identity in *Fin-de-Siècle* Vienna", PhD Dissertation, University of California at San Diego, 1997/Ann Arbor: (UMI) 1997, pp. 159–163.

12 Margaret Olin has made a detailed effort to link Riegl's shift of career to the specific institutional and political context of *fin-de-siècle* Vienna. She highlights that Riegl's intervention in the infected debate on the restoration of Vienna Cathedral took place shortly before his appointment at the Central Commission and argues that it contributed to him being appointed as Director, see Olin, Margaret, "The Cult of Monuments as a State Religion in late 19th Century Austria", *Wiener Jahrbuch für Kunstgeschichte*, 38, 1985, pp. 177–198.

13 Riegl's article "Das Riesenthor zu St. Stephan", in *Neue Freie Presse*, February 1902, republished in Bacher Ernst, *Kunstwerk oder Denkmal? Alois Riegls Schriften zur Denkmalpflege*, Wien, Köln and Weimar: Böhlau Verlag, 1995, pp. 147–156.

14 I follow here closely Margaret Olin's record of the debate as put forward in her article, "The Cult of Monuments as a State Religion in late 19th Century Austria", *Wiener Jahrbuch für Kunstgeschichte*, 38, 1985, pp. 177–198.

15 The 'scrape versus anti-scrape' debate dominated nineteenth century restoration and has remained central to the literature on restoration in the twentieth century. 'Scrape' is associated with the idea of 'unity of style', which aims at restoring monuments to their former glory; 'anti-scrape' is associated with an antiquarian theory which seeks to preserve buildings in the condition that time has bestowed upon them. See Tschudi-Madsen, Stephan, *Restoration and Anti-Restoration*, Oslo: Universitetförlaget, 1976; Denslagen, Wim, *Architectural Restoration in Western Europe: Controversy and Continuity*, Amsterdam: Architectura & Natura Press, 1994; Kåring, Göran, *När medeltidens sol gått ned*, Stockholm: Kungl. Vitterhets Historie och Antikvitets Akademien, 1992.

16 Similar phrases and terminology can be found in the proposed legislation and the essay, and it is most likely that Riegl himself drafted the law although this was published anonymously by the Central Commission for Artistic and Historical Monuments in Vienna, 1903. The law is republished in Bacher, Ernst, *Kunstwerk oder Denkmal? Alois Riegls Schriften zur Denkmalpflege*, Wien, Köln and Weimar: Böhlau Verlag, 1995, pp. 117–120.

17 The *Venice Charter* is the agreed text of the definitions and aims of conservation approved at the Second International Conference of Architects and Technicians of Historic Monuments in Venice 1964. For the relation between the draft legislation and the Venice Charter see Bacher, Ernst, *Kunstwerk oder Denkmal? Alois Riegls Schriften zur Denkmalpflege*, Wien, Köln and Weimar: Böhlau Verlag, 1995, p. 40.

18 In Riegl, Alois, "The Modern Cult of Monuments", p. 21, a similar definition of the monument is used as that in the first paragraph of the proposed legislation drafted most probably by Alois Riegl. See Bacher, Ernst, *Kunstwerk oder Denkmal? Alois Riegls Schriften zur Denkmalpflege*, Wien, Köln and Weimar: Böhlau Verlag, 1995, p. 117.

19 Riegl, Alois, "The Modern Cult of Monuments", p. 21.

20 Riegl, Alois, "The Modern Cult of Monuments", pp. 21–23.

21 Riegl, Alois, "The Modern Cult of Monuments", p. 21.

22 Riegl, Alois, "The Modern Cult of Monuments", p. 24.

23 Riegl, Alois, "The Modern Cult of Monuments", p. 23.

24 Riegl, Alois, "The Modern Cult of Monuments", pp. 24–31. See also Choay, Françoise, *L'allégorie du patrimoine*, Paris: Seuil, 1992, pp. 128–131. Choay follows Riegl's account of the history of conservation but emphasises the crucial contribution of the French Revolution in disseminating the notion of heritage. Choay traces the activities of the humanists and sees their interest in history and the rediscovery of antiquity as the beginning of the formation of a new concept; the *historical* monument. This thesis, on the other hand, has emphasised the discontinuity between a Renaissance notion of heritage, in which the continuity with Antiquity was emphasised, and the ideas of the French Revolution which for the first time used conservation to break with rather than to connect to the past.

25 Riegl, Alois, "The Modern Cult of Monuments", p. 24.

26 I would like to thank Mark Cousins for pointing this out to me.

27 Riegl, Alois, "The Modern Cult of Monuments", p. 32.

28 Riegl, Alois, "The Modern Cult of Monuments", pp. 21–31.

29 Use-value related primarily to architectural structures, but could also include the safety measures taken in relation to other types of monument. The principal is that the monuments should not risk damaging an onlooker (falling stones etc.).Riegl, Alois, "The Modern Cult of Monuments", pp. 39–42.

30 Riegl, Alois, "The Modern Cult of Monuments", pp. 20–24 and further "The Main Characteristics of the Late Roman *Kunstwollen*", conclusion of Riegl, Alois, *Late Roman Art Industry*, trans. Rolf Winkes, Rome: Bretschneider, 1985 pp. 223–234. (Conclusion also reprinted in Wood, Christopher, S, ed., *The Vienna School Reader: Politics and Art Historical Method in the 1930s*, New York: Zone Books, 2000, pp. 87–98.) For a discussion of Riegl's concept of *Kunstwollen* see, Iversen, Margaret, *Alois Riegl: Art History and Theory*, Cambridge, MA, and London: MIT Press, 1993 pp. 3–18. Iversen emphasises Hegel's impact on Riegl's theory of art. This is refuted by Diana Reynolds, who defines a different background for Riegl's idea of *Kunstwollen*, emphasising the impact of Schopenhauer and Nietzsche. See Reynolds, Diana Graham, "Alois Riegl and the Politics of Art History: Intellectual Traditions and Austrian Identity in *Fin-de-Siècle* Vienna", PhD Dissertation, University of California at San Diego, 1997/Ann Arbor: (UMI) 1997, pp. 26–69. See also Olin, Margaret, *Forms of Representation in Alois Riegl's Theory of Art*, University Park, Pennsylvania: Pennsylvania State University Press, 1992, specifically pp. 148–153. The most comprehensive study of Riegl's notion of *Kunstwollen* in relation to the history of modern architecture is Anders Munch's book on Adolf Loos' architecture and its cultural background. See, Munch,

Anders, V., *Den Stilløse Stil: Adolf Loos*, Kunstakademiets Arkitektskoles Forlag, 2002, see specifically the chapter "De moderne nerver og det moderna kunstsyn-Riegl", pp 153–178.

31 Riegl, Alois, "The Modern Cult of Monuments", p. 42. Kurt W Forster has argued that Riegl never identified the aesthetic category of the fragment; on the other hand an interesting vagueness is present in Riegl's schema: it remains unclear if age-value is just a commemorative-value or if it is also an aesthetic property of the object. For Forster's comment on the fragment in Riegl's theory see Forster, Kurt W, "Monument/Memory and the Mortality of Architecture", *Oppositions*, 25, fall 1982, p. 10.

32 Riegl, Alois, "The Modern Cult of Monuments", p. 24.

33 Riegl, Alois, "The Modern Cult of Monuments", p. 48.

34 Riegl, Alois, "The Modern Cult of Monuments", p. 44.

35 For Riegl's criticism of historicism, see Reynolds, Diana Graham, "Alois Riegl and the Politics of Art History: Intellectual Traditions and Austrian Identity in *Fin-de-Siècle* Vienna", PhD Dissertation, University of California at San Diego/Ann Arbor: (UMI) 1997.

36 Riegl, Alois, "The Modern Cult of Monuments", p. 42. For the reference to Siegfreid Giedion, see Giedion, Siegfreid, *Mechanization Takes Command: a Contribution to Anonymous History* (1948), repub., New York and London: Norton, 1969, pp. 607–611.

37 Riegl, Alois "The Modern Cult of Monuments", pp. 43–44.

38 For Riegl's criticism of historicism, see Reynolds, Diana Graham, "Alois Riegl and the Politics of Art History: Intellectual Traditions and Austrian Identity in *Fin-de-Siècle* Vienna", PhD Dissertation, University of California at San Diego, 1997, Ann Arbor (UMI) 1997.

39 Riegl, Alois, "The Modern Cult of Monuments", p. 44.

40 Although it can be argued that *cult* in English gives more associations to religion than the German term *Kultus* that Riegl uses, in a later essay, "Neue Strömungen", he develops the association between religion and "the cult of monuments". See, Riegl, Alois, "Neue Stömungen", 1905, republished in Bacher Ernst, *Kunstwerk oder Denkmal? Alois Riegls Schriften zur Denkmalpflege*, Wien, Köln and Weimar: Böhlau Verlag, 1995. For a critique of the Forster/Ghirardo translation of "The Modern Cult of Monuments' see Witt, Inken, and "Der moderne Denkmalkultus Sein Wesen und seine Entstehung", MA dissertation, Architectural Association, London, 1997.

41 Riegl, Alois, "The Modern Cult of Monuments", p. 34.

42 Riegl, Alois, "The Modern Cult of Monuments", p. 48.

43 Riegl, Alois, "The Modern Cult of Monuments", p. 47.

44 Riegl, Alois, "The Modern Cult of Monuments", pp. 22–23.

45 See Carl E. Schorske's now classic book "*Fin-de-Siècle Vienna, Politics and Culture*" for an account of the shifting political climate in turn of the century Vienna (Schorske, Carl, E, *Fin-de-Siècle Vienna, Politic and Culture*, (1961) repub. New York: Random House, 1981).

RESTORATION IN THE MACHINE AGE

The research for this book took its somewhat unlikely start in a study of Le Corbusier's *Urbanisme*, 1925. I was intrigued by the rhetoric in one of its chapters, *"Le 'Plan Voisin' de Paris et le Passé"*, in which Le Corbusier justified his radical scheme to modernise Paris with the assertion that it would save the past.[1] This statement from an architect whose urban strategies have so strongly been connected to the destruction of heritage seemed dubious and made me curious to explore further how Le Corbusier meant that his plan for Paris could safeguard the past. This chapter will discuss conservation's position as a visual trope in modernity in relation to Le Corbusier's canonical scheme for modernising Paris; the Plan Voisin from 1925. In the plan, which has been described as a *tabula rasa*, Le Corbusier intended to preserve a group of historical monuments and at the same time render the city thoroughly modern. The monuments, signifying the essence of Paris, were to stand in a park created through the erasure of the urban fabric. This has been noted by critics from Reyner Banham but has usually been regarded as either expedient or ironic.[2] Yet the presence of these monuments is significant in as much as it indicates a linked strategy of conservation and destruction at work, suggesting both the idolatry and iconoclasm implicit in the modern cult of monuments at the beginning of the twentieth century.[3]

MODERNITY AND RESTORATION

In *Quand les cathédrales étaient blanches*, 1937, Le Corbusier makes one of his few direct comments on the discipline of restoration:

> The old church, Saint-Étienne de la Cité, has not been 'renovated' or 'restored' by the services of the Office of Historic Monuments. That care was reserved for the Church of Saint Front Saint-Étienne, left in its destitution, is admirable and disturbing; Saint Front, violated by restorers, is henceforth lost. I believe in the

Le Corbusier and Monsieur
De Monzie in front of the
panorama of the Ville
Contemporaine exhibited
in the Esprit Nouveau
pavilion in the Exposition
des Arts Décoratif, Paris,
1925. Photograph.
Fondation Le Corbusier.
Copyright FLC/Adagp, Paris/
BONO, Oslo 2011.

skin of things, as in that of women. At Saint Front they have scraped everything, retouched, *remade*, inch by inch. They have falsified everything: liars; forgers. By what right? Tragic confusion! I know perfectly well that their intentions were good. Alas, alas![4]

Later in the same book Le Corbusier totally reverses his attitude:

I visited the museum in Vicenza where a miracle greeted me. A fearless curator had cleaned everything in the museum, completely. The centuries were destroyed; the painting was fresh as if of yesterday. It was a revelation. The curator told me: 'Yes, I scraped everything, took everything off. The works are as they were made.' Now that was a strength.[5]

The first passage expresses a strong sensation, one that is almost erotic ("admirable and disturbing"). This emotion contrasts with that of the second passage, in which the fascination with time is replaced by a desire to bring the past into the present. This inconsistency on Le Corbusier's part points to the very distinction between age-value and historical-value, identified by Alois Riegl in 1903.[6] In Le Corbusier's emotional response to Saint-Étienne, the value of age, which gives the church a human dimension of mortality, is the primary concern. Ruskinian in his protest against restoration, Le Corbusier emphasised the visual surface, the patina of the building.[7]

Visuality is also the motive for Le Corbusier's desire to see the paintings restored to their original state, but here with a radically different objective. He wants to *see* the paintings released from the shadow of age. Patina is now an obstacle to historical truth rather than a source of visual pleasure:

Throughout the world works of art were made to lie. The great, courageous artists of all periods were shown to us falsely, under a thick layer of dirt accumulated for centuries. Patina! Distinguished, reassuring, calming, emollient patina, very much in harmony with the dark buildings and the false taste of the interiors.[8]

These two contradictory ocular desires expressed in *Quand les cathédrales étaient blanches* resonate with the conflicting values directing conservation at the turn of the twentieth century. However for Le Corbusier, whether the reconstruction or preservation the object is at stake, issues of representation and visuality come to the fore. Taken together these diverging conservation strategies, which manifest themselves through alternative ways of looking at the past, can be read as a kind of modernisation of the heritage object that is brought into the realm of the modern under the aegis of visuality.

LE "PLAN VOISIN" DE PARIS ET LE PASSÉ

Le Corbusier's project *La Ville Contemporaine* has become an emblem of the modernist city created *ex nihilo*. It shows an urban landscape characterised by the repetition of uniform skyscrapers, elaborately separated traffic flows, and vast open spaces. But while presented as an abstract, universally applicable model Le Corbusier's scheme clearly had from its inception a close relationship to Paris.[9]

The programme for the project emerged through his analysis of the problems of post-war Paris: increasing congestion, poor housing and a lack of office space. When exhibited at the Salon d'Automne of 1922, the Ville Contemporaine was accompanied by a sketch showing, as a 'concrete case', its effect on the historical centre of Paris, together with a manifesto for the future of the city:

> **Paris expects of this age: the rescue of its endangered way of life, the safe-keeping of its beautiful past, the magnificent and powerful demonstration of the spirit of the 20th century....[10]**

Three years later, at the 1925 *Exposition des Arts Décoratifs* in Paris, the 'concrete case', now baptized "Voisin" after its patron, the automobile manufacturer Gabriel Voisin, dominated the exhibit.[11]

In the exhibition the Plan Voisin was presented as the solution to an urgent problem: that of saving Paris from the dangerous forces of modernity that were threatening both the future of the city and, significantly, its past. While several aspects of the scheme were reflected in later urban planning, Le Corbusier's claim that it would preserve the past was not taken up. On the contrary, from its inauguration the Plan Voisin was criticised for its brutal effect upon Paris' historical centre.[12] Indeed, in the history of urbanism the Plan has often stood as a symbol of the Modern Movement's dismissive attitude towards the past.[13] However the objective of saving the past in the Voisin scheme is intriguing in the sense that it reveals the preservation of historical structures as a crucial component within the discourse of Modernist planning represented here by Le Corbusier's canonical scheme.

For the 1925 Art Deco exhibition the editors of *L'Esprit Nouveau* were invited to construct a pavilion illustrating the theme "An Architect's House".[14] Le Corbusier responded to the brief by choosing to exhibit the Plan Voisin in its entirety, from the intimate scale of interior decoration to the scheme's effect on Paris as a whole.[15] The project was communicated through the realisation at full scale of one of its basic components, a housing unit from the Immeuble-Villas, the large apartment blocks composed of maisonettes, which were to be placed along the perimeter of the business centre. Furnished—or, as Le Corbusier preferred to call it, equipped—

Exterior view of the L'Esprit
Nouveau pavilion showing
the rotunda that contained
the panoramas, Exposition
des Arts Décoratif, Paris,
1925, Photograph.

Published in *Oeuvre Complète*,
1910–1929. Copyright FLC/Adagp,
Paris/BONO, Oslo 2011.

Interior view of the
rotunda in the L'Esprit
Nouveau pavilion, showing,
on the right, the Ville
Contemporaine, and on the
left Plan Voisin, Exposition
des Arts Décoratif, Paris,
1925. Photograph.

Fondation Le Corbusier.
Copyright FLC/Adagp, Paris/
BONO, Oslo 2011.

Panorama of the Ville
Contemporaine, as
exhibited in the Esprit
Nouveau pavilion, Paris,
1925. Drawing/print.
Fondation Le Corbusier.
Copyright FLC/Adagp, Paris/
BONO, Oslo 2011.

this "standardised cell" was a modern, urban dwelling in every respect. Le Corbusier
even constructed an appropriate view for the apartment in the form of an enormous
panorama of the Voisin scheme.

> **I painted a panorama whose aim was to make evident to the eye this new
> conception, so unfamiliar to us as yet. The panorama was most carefully
> executed and showed Paris as it is today, from Notre-Dame to the Étoile,
> including those monuments which are our imperishable heritage. Behind
> it rose the new city.[16]**

The panorama was exhibited on one side of a rotunda attached to the maisonette unit, an
extension which occupied nearly half the plan area of the Pavillon de l'Esprit Nouveau.
Opposite the Voisin panorama was displayed its conceptual origin, the Ville Contemporaine.
These panoramas, with their lack of a fixed vanishing point, allowed the viewer an
ambulatory ubiquity; strolling in front of them the Parisians could familiarise themselves
with the possible future of their city. In this familiarisation the historical monuments of the
city played a crucial role, constituting the main difference between the two panoramas. The
"laboratory work" of the Ville Contemporaine presented an abstract city; the Plan Voisin,
with its familiar historical monuments, returned the spectator to Paris.

Panorama of the Plan
Voisin with the monuments
in the foreground, as
exhibited in the Esprit
Nouveau pavilion, Paris,
1925. Drawing/print.
Fondation Le Corbusier.
Copyright FLC/Adagp, Paris/
BONO, Oslo 2011

The sophistication of these panoramas finds a parallel in the penthouse Le Corbusier designed in 1929 for Charles de Beistegui. Situated on the rooftop of a building in the Avenue des Champs-Élysées, high above the centre of Paris, this project, like the Pavillon de l'Esprit Nouveau, operated as a prototype for the Plan Voisin. The penthouse, particularly its roof garden, was an intriguing instrument for viewing a set of monuments selected to represent the essence of Paris. Tall hedges, clipped with geometric precision, denied the possibility of a full panoramic view over the city. Instead, four openings in this "green wall" framed views, in turn, of the Arc de Triomphe, the Eiffel Tower, Sacré Coeur, and Notre-Dame.[17]

In the Beistegui scheme, which Le Corbusier later described as a paradigm of his urban principles, historical Paris, with its rundown and congested streets, was blocked out in favour of selected monuments. The Plan Voisin envisaged the *literal* demolition of the same city fabric that the Bestigui apartment screened off. This area, described by Le Corbusier in *Urbanisme* as the "particularly antiquated and unhealthy part of Paris, i.e. from the Place de la République to the Rue du Louvre, and from the Gare de l'Est to the Rue de Rivoli", was to be replaced by the commercial centre of the project. The new residential district would have extended the destruction even further, to the district between the Rue des Pyramides, the circus on the Champs Élysées, and the Gare Saint-Lazare.[18] However, in the chapter "Le 'Plan Voisin' de Paris et le Passé" Le Corbusier makes the following claim:

Photograph of the
garden of the Beistegui
penthouse, Paris 1930–
1931, showing the view
of the Arc de Triomphe.
Published in Le Corbusier,
Oeuvre Complète de 1929–1934.
Copyright FLC/Adagp, Paris/
BONO, Oslo 2011

In this scheme the historical past, our common inheritance, is respected. More than that, it is rescued. The persistence of the present state of crisis must otherwise lead rapidly to the destruction of that past.[19]

In the Plan Voisin this past is represented by a collection of monuments, shown highlighted in red on the plan drawings of the project.[20] In general the Plan Voisin can be seen to follow the nineteenth century tradition of "cleansing" the monument of all accretions. Among the churches that were to be preserved as isolated structures are Saint-Eustache, Saint-Nicholas des Champs, Sainte-Elisabeth, Saint-Leu-Saint-Gille, Sainte-Marie Madeleine, and Saint-Augustin. Institutional buildings such as the Opéra, the Bourse and the Bibliothèque Nationale, although they belonged to the academic tradition of the Beaux Arts that Le Corbusier despised, were to be treated in a similar fashion. The Port Saint-Denis and Port Saint-Martin were also to be rescued, and loosely fitted into the overall composition. They appear on the vast main square of the scheme, occupying it like two obelisks, although they are not aligned with the grid—a topographical dislocation which betrays their past.[21]

Writing on the Plan Voisin and the historical monuments Stanislaus von Moos suggests that Le Corbusier's Plan Voisin was in fact a radical version of Haussmann's clearance and conservation of Paris' historic landmarks.[22] This is an acute observation pointing to the 'tradition' within Le Corbusier's scheme. However, an important difference between Haussmann's approach to the monuments and that of Le Corbusier should be noted. In the Voisin scheme the monuments (with the exception of Port St Dennis and Port St Martin) are detached from the traffic infrastructure, carefully dislocated by their placement in the park; in the Haussmann project, the ancient monuments participate as landmarks in the new infrastructure of Paris. Indeed, none of the existing monuments seems to have affected the monumental grid of the Voisin scheme.

This is also true of the 'voids' that Le Corbusier preserves. The Palais Royal, Place Vendôme and Place de la Madeleine appear preserved as "enclosed spaces" rather than conventional monuments. The arcades of the Rue de Rivoli which line the Tuileries and the *hôtels* that line the Place de la Concorde also stand detached, severed from the urban fabric that once defined them. These canonical examples are all cited in *Urbanisme*, to show how demolition has successfully been used in the past to create distinctive urban forms. At one level these historical 'model' urban ensembles created out of destruction were crucial archival references for the Voisin scheme and therefore needed to be saved at the same time as they contradicted the law of historical determinism: "... in the name of History, according to the laws of History, to the moral of History and the lesson of History, an old city must always be replaced by a new city."[23]

Le Corbusier. Plan-
drawing of the Plan Voisin
showing the selected
monuments highlighted
in red as published in
Urbanisme, 1925.

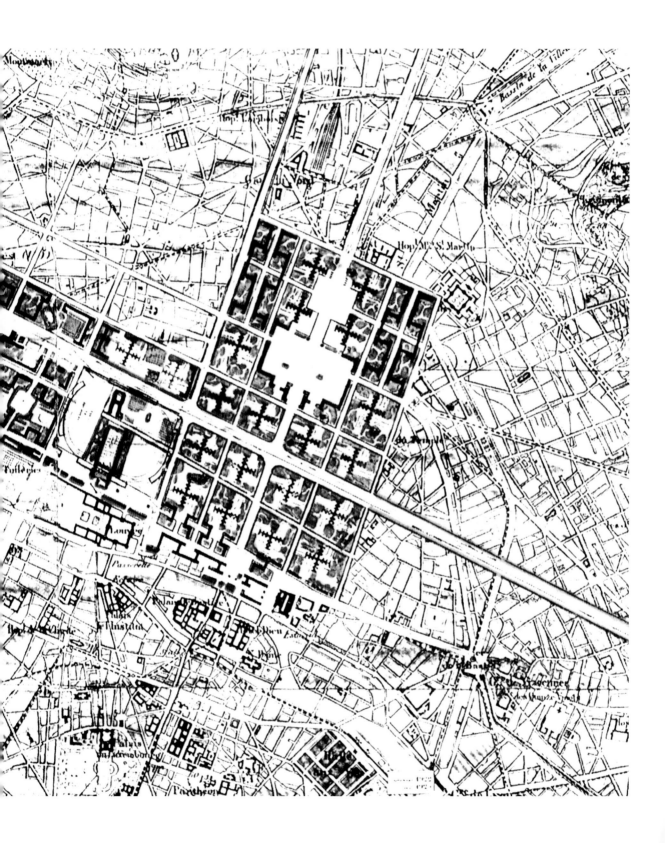

This collection of certain key spaces from the historical city, where the voids, rather than the physical structures that define them, are the object of conservation signals a different approach to urban preservation from that taken elsewhere in the scheme.[24] It shows clearly how Le Corbusier envisaged the park in the Plan Voisin to work as a museum for the city. As the historical accounts in *Urbanisme* and *Vers une architecture* show, Le Corbusier considered old town centres valuable as historical models, but owing to their permanence and a-temporality he also considered them as a dangerous challenge to modern urban planning: if the new were to be inserted into the old, the result would be chaos.[25] Manfredo Tafuri, suggests that this danger arose for Le Corbusier from the value of permanence represented by the built structures of old cities, particularly when contrasted with the rapid pace of life in the modern city.[26] This ambivalence in Le Corbusier's appreciation of historical cities leaves as the only alternative to radical destruction the "museographic mummification" of the historical remains of the city, turning them into "silent museums", in Tafuri's words.

It is necessary to develop Tafuri's analysis, however. For Le Corbusier the danger of the past goes beyond the conflict between permanence and transience to the issue of the need for history. History offers modern man a necessary, though dangerous, lesson.[27] The chapter "La Leçon de Rome" in *Vers une architecture*, 1923, ends with his famous attack on the French Academy: "The lesson of Rome is for wise men, for those who know and can appreciate, who can resist and can verify.... To send architectural students to Rome is to cripple them for life."[28] This Nietzschean remark about the danger of history returns in a slightly different version in *L'Art décoratif d'aujourd'hui*, 1925, when he discuss the museum:

> The museums are a means of instruction for the most intelligent, just as the city of Rome is a fruitful lesson for those who have a profound knowledge of their craft.[29]

There is a latent analogy here between the danger of the historical city and that of the museum. The danger Le Corbusier attributes to the museum arises from its tendency to exhibit 'rubbish', its failure to exercise discrimination, its undermining of historical progress by juxtaposing in space objects from different periods. Confronted with a 'heap' of historical objects, the critical faculties are easily lost, encouraging unquestioning admiration of the past.[30] Thus his attack on the institution of the museum in the chapter "Autres Icones, Les Musées": "The museum is bad because it does not tell the whole story. It misleads, it dissimulates, it deludes. It is a liar."[31] Yet Le Corbusier does not despise the museum *per se*; indeed, he emphasises its potential role as a paradigm of the law of historical development: "The museum reveals the full story, and it is therefore good: it allows one to choose, to accept or reject."[32] Rearranged so as to present "the complete picture after the passage of time, after the destruction by time", the museum offers the necessary opportunity to understand why things are as they are.[33] Indeed, it is the museum itself which makes possible the modern:

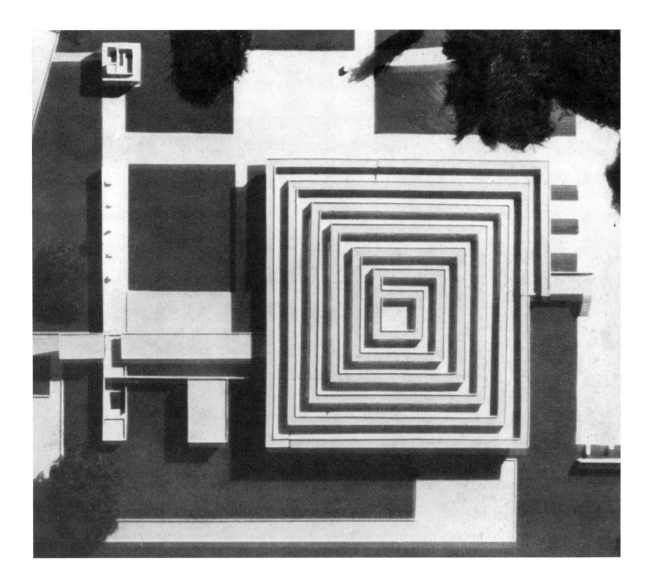

Le Corbusier. Bird's-eye view of "A Museum for Unlimited Growth", 1939.
Published in *Oeuvre Complète*, 1938–1946. Copyright FLC/Adagp, Paris/BONO, Oslo 2011.

True enough, there is good in the museum; but let us risk a devastating deduction: the museum allows one to reject it all, because once the full story is known, it becomes clear that everything has its time and place and that nothing from the past is directly of use to us. For our life on this world is a path on which we can never retrace our steps.[34]

This idea is reflected in the several designs Le Corbusier made for an unlimited museum, all based on the principle of an extended spiral. The spatial organisation of these projects is linear; as the visitor moves through the museum, time unfolds and the history of human achievement is explained.[35]

However, while the museum could be organised according to a linear narrative, to explain historical development through a city's monuments demands a more complex structure. This is illustrated in a series of drawings made for a lecture in Buenos Aires in 1929, used by Le Corbusier to defend his scheme for Paris. The drawings formed an 'architectural strip' depicting the evolution of Paris from the Middle Ages to the present. Each historical period is represented by a monument: Notre-Dame, the Louvre, Les Invalides, the Pantheon, the Eiffel Tower. On the final strip Le Corbusier incorporated his own contribution to the history of the city, the skyscrapers of the Voisin scheme. He ended his text accompanying the images with a plea: "I beg Paris to make, once more, its historical gesture: to continue."[36]

Le Corbusier's strip suggests at once the passage of time and its suspension: each period in history is represented by an image, but monuments from different periods are simultaneously present. The conflict between permanence and change is here a spatial one: Le Corbusier wants to represent the different historical periods in the city evolution but at the same time he wants to render the city truly modern. However, to represent historical sequence in spatial terms can only be done through juxtaposition in space; Medieval Paris cannot exist in the present except as an integral part of modern Paris—Medieval Paris must in fact *be* modern Paris. It was this loss of age, this 'nowness', that disturbed Le Corbusier; writing about the role of the past in the Voisin scheme, he argued that the aim of erasing the urban context was to put an end to such falsification:

> First of all I must make a distinction, of a sentimental nature, but one of great importance; in these days the past has lost something of its fragrance, for its enforced mingling with the life of today has set it in a false environment. My dream is to see the Place de la Concorde empty once more, silent and lonely, and the Champs Élysées a quiet place to walk in. The 'Voisin' scheme would isolate the whole of the ancient city and bring back peace and calm from Saint-Gervais to the Étoile.[37]

Frequently comparing his plan for Paris' historical centre to those of Colbert, Richelieu and Haussmann, Le Corbusier insisted that Paris should remain on its historical site. In *La Ville Radieuse* he repeated this argument: "Paris was transformed on its own ground, without evasion. Each current of thought is inscribed in its stones, throughout the centuries. In this way the living images of Paris were formed. Paris must continue!"[38] This refusal to isolate the historical centre of Paris by locating new buildings on its periphery was central to Le Corbusier's strategy of rescuing the city's past while at the same time rendering it modern.

Le Corbusier.
"Architectural strip"
showing Paris'
historical development.
Published in *Précisions*.
Copyright FLC/Adagp, Paris/
BONO, Oslo 2011.

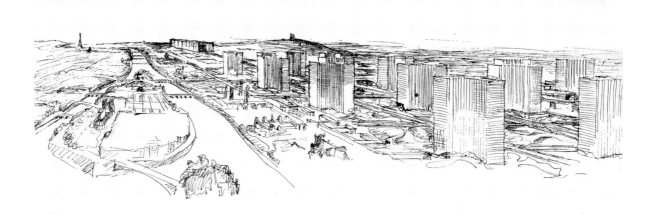

Le Corbusier. Bird's-eye
view of Plan Voisin.
Published in *Oeuvre Complète*,
1910–1929. Copyright FLC/Adagp,
Paris/BONO, Oslo 2011.

ET IN ARCADIA EGO

In his drawings for the new city of the Plan Voisin, Le Corbusier often uses an elevated point of view overlooking an apparently boundless space. In describing the park in the scheme, on the other hand, he puts forward a different image. The endless vistas are exchanged for a picturesque intimacy. Moving through the park at ground level, we encounter 'moments' in the history of architecture: "Here, all of a sudden, one is facing a charming Gothic church, cradled in greenery: there are Saint-Martin or Saint-Merry of the fourteenth or fifteenth centuries."[39] This series of carefully framed heritage vignettes even included the monuments of the future: "Through the branches, rising behind the hills that seem like the distant views in a film, one sees the crystal prisms of the immense office buildings."[40] While vision is the sense in question here, it is striking how Le Corbusier underlines the immediate, tactile presence of the historical monuments, in opposition to the abstract distance of the skyscrapers. While the former seem to have found their 'true place' within the park, the new is left outside.

The organisation of the new city played a decisive role in this strategy. Streets were replaced by elevated terraces two or three storeys above ground level. Lined with cafes, shops, clubs and restaurants, they were to assume both the social and the commercial functions of the street. Raised on pillars and interconnected by a system of elevated motorways, the skyscrapers of the business centre were also to be removed from the ground: "Crystal that reflects the sky, that shines in the grey skies of winter, that seems rather to float in the air than stand on the ground."[41]

The parkland that lies beneath the city was then carefully isolated from the forces of modern life, the very forces that had conditioned the Voisin scheme: "A city made for speed is made for success... if we do not produce, we die."[42] In that sense the park constituted the antithesis of the city and worked as a table of memory rather than as a *tabula rasa*. In the Arcadian park the remains of the pre-modern city could be displayed for the citizens without the disturbance of the new:

> ... still standing among the masses of foliage of the new parks, certain historical monuments, arcades, doorways, carefully preserved because they are pages out of history or works of art.[43]

In the name of history Le Corbusier had argued that the old city needed to be replaced with a new.

> Paris of the past, yet still close to us.... Poetry of yesteryear, now destroyed. Sacrilege, don't you agree? So it's happened to us in the past, and other things too will die, like these, when they have outlived their reason for being.[44]

Le Corbusier conceived of the historical centre of Paris in nearly archaeological terms; as a site of both destruction and reconstruction.[45] Beneath the new city the past would lay out its remains, exposed to descending visitors as if in an open grave: "I say 'below-ground', but it would be more exact to say at what we call basement level, for if my town, built on concrete piles, were realised, this 'basement' would no longer be buried under earth."[46] The monuments, excavated from the urban topography and released from the flux of modernity were rendered permanent. Fragmented and reframed, the past in this setting would no longer obstruct modern life. Crucially a distance had been established between the historical objects and their observers, ending the "enforced mingling with the life of today" that Le Corbusier saw as so harmful to modern man as well as the historical monuments themselves. Removed from the normal economic forces of society the monuments in the park were thus conserved for the eye; like objects in a museum they now belonged to the recreation of the Sunday:

> The 'Voisin' scheme covers five per cent only of the ground with buildings, it safeguards the relics of the past and enshrines them harmoniously in a framework of trees and woods. For material things too must die, and these green parks with their relics are in some sort cemeteries, carefully tended, in which people may breathe, dream and learn. In this way the past becomes no longer dangerous to life, but finds instead its true place within it.[47]

DISPLACING THE PAST

The true place for the past is the museum: the Voisin park, if not literally a walled museum, shared with the museum a distinctive condition of displacement. The mechanism of Le Corbusier's saving of the past in Paris can be considered in light of the analyses of the previous chapters in this book. In Alexander Lenoire's Petits-Augustins and my analysis of the Revolutionary museum, for example, it became clear how a complex past was removed from the city and saved as history in a space that was both literally and semantically apart from the urban realm. Equally in Plan Voisin this strategy of displacement should be understood not as expedient or cynical but as in a fundamental way, required. This aspect of Plan Voisin shows that, in contradistinction to Viollet-le-Duc whose reconstructions brought monuments into the present and made them contiguous with the space of the contemporary city, for Le Corbusier the rescue of the past relied on a fundamental act of spatial displacement. In a passage from "The Modern Cult of Monuments" on the conflict between use and conservation Riegl makes a suggestion that anticipates Plan Voisin's museological strategy of both saving and removing the monuments from the use of the everyday: "Assume that it was actually possible to replace all monuments still in use so that they would be allowed to live out their natural life although without any practical utility". [48] Le Corbusier's proposal for re-building Paris can be read as an almost literal embodiment of Riegl's suggestion, rendering possible the saving of the past within the modern through spatial dislocation.

Le Corbusier had argued that in the 'name of history' the old city must be replaced by a new. Regardless of performance or age nothing of the old city was of use. The old city could not without danger be a place for production and could only be saved by being removed from the everyday. Plan Voisin is early in calling for the designation of a specific space for the past within the modern city shaped by the forces of capitalism, a requirement that was to become familiar in later and contemporary conservationist strategies that aim to save the past by classifying it as distinct from the present—historic districts, historical areas and historical regions.

Le Corbusier ends the chapter "Le 'Plan Voisin' de Paris et le Passé" in *Urbanisme* with the remark that the Voisin scheme does not claim to have found the definitive solution to the re-planning of Paris. But he suggests that the project will nevertheless raise the discussion to a level worthy of the time: "It [the Voisin scheme] sets up principles as against the medley of silly little reforms with which we are constantly deceiving ourselves."[50] Nearly a century later heritage legislation is one of the strongest forces determining the physical form and the visual identity of cities, landscapes and regions worldwide. Le Corbusier's act of displacing of the past has resonance with the strategies of conservation that result from the regulatory frameworks of heritage, particularly the development of Unesco's World Heritage List. Today these codes governing World Heritage sites create a meta-structure through the action of "listing", a space that is conceptually related to the park in Plan Voisin, but infinitely larger in scope, stretching through different time-zones, climates and cultures.

When the research in this chapter was originally published (in *AA Files* 1999) the ironies implicit in this identity between the strategies of conservation and those of modernism

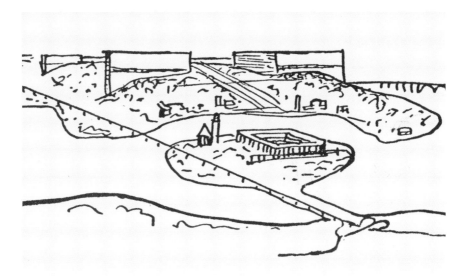

Le Corbusier.
Plan for Stockholm.
Published in *Oeuvre
Complète*, 1929–1934.
Copyright FLC/Adagp, Paris/
BONO, Oslo 2011.

were most apparent. The UK debates around Prince Charles' critique of modern architecture, his move into conservation and urban regeneration, assumed a categorical divide between the ideals of modern architecture and those informed by historical architecture and conservation.[49] At that time it was felt necessary to challenge this opposition, and the article therefore underlined the modernity of conservation and pointed to the close relationships between modernistic urban planning and the discourse on the historical monument.

Revisiting the text now, when the notion of historical urban areas has become ubiquitous and participates in the branding and marketing of the European city, another aspect of the argument is more urgent to lift forward. The crucial point here, and specifically in relation to Le Corbusier's modernisation plans for Paris, is that the use and the symbolic function of that which is saved becomes a secondary issue. The value of the monument lies not in its performance as an economic or spatial resource, or in its representation of national identity, but in its therapeutic capacity at times of rapid societal change.

During the 1930s Le Corbusier participated in the competition for the modernisation of the city of Stockholm in Sweden. His proposal identified the city's Old Town as a monument to be saved in its entirety, while the rest of the existing city was to be replaced by meandering mega-structures, similar to those in Plan Voisin. According to local legend, apart from a radical piece of traffic engineering recently completed south of the Old Town at 'Slussen', Le Corbusier was most impressed by the open-air museum at Skansen in Stockholm. Skansen was one of the world's first open-air museums. Created in the 1890s, Skansen exhibited vernacular buildings from regional Sweden in a parkland setting close to the rapidly developing city; by the 1930s Skansen had expanded its exhibits to save groups of buildings that had become redundant in that development itself. Le Corbusier's appreciation of the open-air museum took place in the context of imagining radical new projections for Stockholm's future, and the model of Skansen as a mechanism for choreographing the simultaneous existence of the past and the future seems powerful. Accounts about Le Corbusier's interest in the open-air museum also circulated in relation to his visit to Oslo during the same period. Here he was drawn to the museum at Bygdøy, Skansen's twin, where he spent a full day in unlicensed solitude, to the consternation of his hosts who had no idea of his whereabouts.

Whatever their origin, these stories point towards the sensibilities Le Corbusier expresses in his descriptions of Plan Voisin. Le Corbusier's arcadian descriptions of the park in Plan Voisin evoke strongly the topos of conservation that developed and found its logic in the open-air museum. In their display of full scale buildings in natural settings, framed by a characteristic mix of the recreational, the sentimental and the academic, open-air museums created a place for a functionally redundant past at a time of rapid urbanisation. Dedicated to vernacular building, and created with urgency to save a culture in change, these early open-air museums in Stockholm and Oslo propelled buildings from the everyday into another space where, as oneric and therapeutic objects, they re-enacted that which was lost in modern urbanised society. In both places the past is translated to a verdant scene of recreation immediately adjacent to, and in the case of Skansen making space for, the rapidly modernising City.

Although the idea of the open-air museum appears now both natural and conservative, there is a radicalism about Skansen and Bygdøy very similar to that which emerges in Le Corbusier's plan to rescue the past in his Paris scheme. The Plan Voisin, like the open-air museum, entertains the notion of architecture as exhibit, at full scale, saving and reframing the past. 'Zoning', usually associated with the separation of functions within the Modernist city plan, is used to create this designated space for the past. In Plan Voisin there is an echo both of the sense of vertiginous speed that formed the context for the invention of the open-air museum—a rapid, sudden change of the pattern of urban habitation—and the requirement for a therapeutic space with which to deal with its effects. Incorporated into the present as redundant and displaced, in this model the past becomes the site of either nostalgia or utopia.

BIBLIOGRAPHICAL SUMMARY

As a one of the most dominant architects in the Modern Movement, Le Corbusier is a well researched figure. Stanislaus von Moos' classic book *Le Corbusier: Elements of a Synthesis* originally published as *Le Corbusier: Elemente einer Synthese*, as well as William Curtis' *Le Corbusier: Ideas and Form* and Richard Etlin's *Frank Lloyd Wright and Le Corbusier: The Romantic Legacy* proved valuable entries into Le Corbusier's thinking on urbanism and architecture (von Moss, Stanislaus, *Le Corbusier: Elements of a Synthesis*, Cambridge, MA: MIT Press, 1979; Curtis, William, *Le Corbusier: Ideas and Form*, Oxford: Phaidon, 1986; Etlin, Richard A, *Frank Lloyd Wright and Le Corbusier: The Romantic Legacy*, Manchester: Manchester University Press, 1994). So were the essays by various scholars in *The Open Hand, Essays on Le Corbusier*, edited by Walden Russell (Walden Russell, ed., *The Open Hand: Essays on Le Corbusier*, Cambridge MA: MIT Press, 1977).

The construction of Le Corbusier as a figure in architectural history, and how this in turn has effected the reading of his urban projects in the context of conservation, was considered in relation to Sigfried Giedion's *Space Time and Architecture* and Reyner Banham's *Theory and Design in the First Machine Age*. (Giedion, Sigfried, *Space, Time and Architecture; The Growth of a New Tradition* (1941), fifth edition, Cambridge, MA: Harvard University Press, 1966, repr., 1995; Banham, Reyner, *Theory and Design in the First Machine Age*, London: The Architectural Press, 1960). For the discussion of Le Corbusier's notion of history and how this influenced his thinking on the museum Paul Turner's *The Education of Le Corbusier* was important as it pointed to the influence on Le Corbusier of Friedrich Nietzsche's criticism of history (Turner, Paul, *The Education of Le Corbusier: A Study of the Development of Le Corbusier's Thought 1900–1920*, New York and London: Garland, 1977).

More specifically Alan Colquhoun's essay "'Newness' and 'Age-Value' in Alois Riegl" was crucial to the chapter's analysis of Plan Voisin and its relation to conservation (Colquhoun, Alan, "'Newness' and 'Age-Value' in Alois Riegl", in *Modernity and the Classical Tradition: Architectural Essays 1980–1987*, Cambridge, MA: MIT Press, 1989). Stanislaus von Moos analysis of the role of the monuments in Le Corbusier's urbanism in "Le Corbusier: The Monument and the Metropolis" and Johan Mårtelius" comments on "Hotet mot Paris" in *Le Corbusier och Stockholm*, have also contributed to my reading of Plan Voisin (von Moos, Stanislaus, "Le Corbusier: The Monument and the Metropolis", *Columbia Documents of Architecture and Theory*, Vol. 3, 1993; Mårtelius, Johan, "Hotet mot Paris", *Le Corbusier och Stockholm*, exhibition catalogue, Stockholm: Arkitekturmuseet, 1987).

Most crucial, however, have been Manfredo Tafuri's observations on Le Corbusier's complex relation to the past structure of the city. His *Theories and History of Architecture* makes short but acute observations on Plan Voisin (Tafuri, Manfredo *Theories and History of Architecture*, New York: Granada, 1976), and his innovative essay "Machine et Mémoire: The City in the Work of Le Corbusier" was important for the chapter's analysis of the Beistegui garden and its relation to Plan Voisin (Tafuri, Manfredo "Machine et Mémoire: The City in the Work of Le Corbusier" in *Le Corbusier*, H Allen Brooks ed., New Jersey: Princeton University Press, 1987). Beatriz Colomina's *Privacy and Publicity: Modern Architecture as Mass Media*, which develops Tafuri's analysis and emphasises the crucial role of vision in Corbusier's urbanism, has also been central for developing the argument. Colomina's elegant analysis of the Beistegui garden has influenced this chapter on an analytical as well as methodological level (Colomina, Beatriz, *Privacy and Publicity: Modern Architecture as Mass Media*, Cambridge, MA: MIT Press, 1994). For the analysis of Alois Riegl's theory of conservation, see the biographical note in Chapter *The Modern Cult of Monument*.

An earlier version of this chapter was published as "Restoration in the Machine Age: Themes of Conservation in Le Corbusier's Plan Voisin", in *AA Files*, 38(1999), pp. 10–22.

PRIMARY SOURCES

Le Corbusier:

Vers une architecture, Paris: G Crès et cie, 1923. Translated as *Towards a New Architecture*, London: The Architectural Press, 1927, revised edition 1931, repr. 1989.

Urbanisme, Paris: G Crès et cie, 1925. Translated as *The City of Tomorrow*, London: The Architectural Press, 1929, repr. 1987.

L'Art décoratif d'aujourd'hui, Paris: G Crès et cie, 1925. Translated as *The Decorative Art of Today*, London: The Architectural Press, 1929, repr. 1987.

La Ville Radieuse, Paris: Éditions de l'Architecture d'Aujourd'hui, 1935. Translated as *The Radiant City*, London: Faber and Faber, 1964.

Précisions sur un état présent de l'architecture et de l'urbanisme, Paris: G Crès et cie, 1930. Translated as *Precisions*, Cambridge, MA: MIT Press, 1991.

Quand les cathédrales étaient blanches, Paris: Plon, 1937. Translated as *When the Cathedrals Were White*, New York: Reynal and Hitchcock, 1942.

Le Corbusier and Pierre Jeanneret:

Oeuvre Complète de 1910–1929, Zurich: Éditions Girsberger, 1937.

Oeuvre Complète de 1938–1946, Zurich: Éditions d'Architecture, Erlenbach, 1946.

Riegl, Alois:

"The Modern Cult of Monuments: Its Character and Its Origin", (Der moderne Denkmalkultus. Sein Wesen und seine Entstehung", Vienna, 1903, republished in *Konservieren, nicht restaurieren. Streitschriften zur Denkmalpflege um 1900*, Braunschweig: Bauwelt Fundamente, Friedr. Vieweg & Sohn, 1988), Kurt Forster and Diane Ghirardo trans., in *Oppositions*, 25, 1982, pp. 21–51.

NOTES

1 Le Corbusier, *Urbanisme*, Paris: G Crès et cie, 1925.

2 Banham, Reyner, *Theory and Design in the First Machine Age*, London: The Architectural Press, 1960, p. 255; Evenson, Norma, *Le Corbusier: The Machine and the Grand Design*, London: Studio Vista, 1974, p. 20; Fishman, Robert, *Urban Utopias in the Twentieth Century*, New York: Basic Books, 1977, pp. 205–212; Curtis, William, *Le Corbusier: Ideas and Form*, Oxford: Phaidon, 1986, p. 64; Hall, Peter, *Cities of Tomorrow: An Intellectual History of Urban Planning and Design in the Twentieth Century*, London: Basil Blackwell, 1988, p. 207.

3 On the Plan Voisin and its relation to conservation strategies, see in particular Manfredo Tafuri (*Theories and History of Architecture*, New York: Granada, 1976, pp. 46–50) who has highlighted the complexity of the presence of the monument in the Plan Voisin in relation to the Modern Movement's anti-historicism and its effect on the preservation of historical towns. See also Alan Colquhoun, "'Newness' and 'Age-Value' in Alois Riegl", in *Modernity and the Classical Tradition: Architectural Essays 1980–1987*, Cambridge, MA: MIT Press, 1989, pp. 213–221, who notes the correspondence between Alois Riegl's theories of conservation and Le Corbusier's preservation of the ancient monuments in the Voisin scheme; and Stanislaus von Moos, "Le Corbusier: The Monument and the Metropolis", *Columbia Documents of Architecture and Theory*, Vol. 3, 1993, pp. 115–137, who has pointed out the role of the monument as such in Le Corbusier's urbanism.

4 Le Corbusier, *When the Cathedrals Were White* (*Quand les cathédrales étaient blanches*, Paris: Plon, 1937), New York: Reynal and Hitchcock, 1942, pp. 13–14.

5 Le Corbusier, *When the Cathedrals Were White*, p. 129.

6 Riegl, Alois, "The Modern Cult of Monuments: Its Character and its Origin", Kurt Forster and Diane Ghirardo trans., *Oppositions*, 25, 1982.

7 See for example John Ruskin's attack on conservation architects in "The Lamp of Memory" in his *The Seven Lamps of Architecture*, 1880, repr. New York: Dover Publications, 1989, p. 196.

8 Le Corbusier, *When the Cathedrals Were White*, p. 128.

9 See further: von Moos, Stanislaus, *Le Corbusier: Elemente einer Synthese*, Zürich: Verlag Hubert & Co, 1968, pp. 179–190.

10 "Paris attend de l'époque: Le sauvetage de sa vie menacée, la sauvegarde de son beau passé, la manifestation magnifique et puissante de l'esprit du XXe siècle." Le Corbusier, *Urbanisme*, Paris: G Crès et cie, 1925, p. 277.

11 For a description of the two exhibitions see: Le Corbusier, Pierre Jeanneret, *Oeuvre Complète de 1910–1929*, Zurich: Éditions Girsberger, 1937, pp. 34–44, 92–104.

12 For further discussion of this criticism, see Evenson, Norma, *Le Corbusier: The Machine and the Grand Design*, London: Studio Vista, 1974.

13 Banham, Reyner, *Theory and Design in the First Machine Age*, London: The Architectural Press, 1960, p. 255; von Moos, Stanislaus, *Le Corbusier: Elemente einer Synthese*, Zürich: Verlag Hubert & Co, 1968, p. 183; Rowe, Colin, and Fred Koetter, *Collage City*, Cambridge, MA: MIT Press, 1973, p. 72; Sennett, Richard, *The Conscience of the Eye: The Design and Social Life of Cities*, London: 1990, Faber and Faber, pp. 170–171.

14 Le Corbusier, *The City of Tomorrow* (*Urbanisme*, Paris: G Crès et cie, 1925), London: The Architectural Press, 1929, repr. 1987, p. 231. Le Corbusier and Pierre Jeanneret, *Oeuvre Complète de 1910–1929*, Zurich: Éditions Girsberger, 1937, pp. 92–104.

15 Le Corbusier, *The City of Tomorrow* (*Urbanisme*, Paris: G Crès et cie, 1925), London: The Architectural Press, 1929, repr. 1987, p. 281.

16 Le Corbusier and Pierre Jeanneret, *Œuvre Complète de 1910–1929*, Zurich: Éditions Girsberger, 1937, Vol. 2 (1930–1934), pp. 53–57.

17 For a fuller description of the Beistegui garden see: Imbert, Dorothée, *The Modernist Garden in France*, New Haven and London: Yale University Press, 1993, pp. 52–73; see also Benton, Tim, *The Villas of Le Corbusier 1920–1930*, New Haven and London: Yale University Press, 1987, p. 209. For an analysis of the role of the city in relation to the penthouse, see Tafuri, Manfredo, "Machine et Mémoire: The City in the Work of Le Corbusier", in *Le Corbusier*, H Allen Brooks ed., New Jersey: Princeton University Press, 1987; von Moos, Stanislaus, "Le Corbusier: The Monument and the Metropolis", *Columbia Documents of Architecture and Theory*, Vol. 3, 1993, pp. 115–137; Colomina, Beatriz, *Privacy and Publicity: Modern Architecture as Mass Media*, Cambridge, MA: MIT Press, 1994, pp. 301–306.

18 Le Corbusier, *The City of Tomorrow*, pp. 277–278.

19 Le Corbusier, *The City of Tomorrow*, p. 287.

20 In the early editions of the English translation the plan of the Voisin scheme was also printed in colour, showing the monuments highlighted in red. See Le Corbusier, *The City of Tomorrow*, p. 276.

21 Le Corbusier, *The City of Tomorrow*, pp. 268–269.

22 von Moos, Stanislaus, "Le Corbusier: The Monument and the Metropolis", *Columbia Documents of Architecture and Theory*, Vol. 3, 1993, p. 128.

23 Le Corbusier, *The Radiant City* (*La Ville Radieuse*, Paris: Éditions de l'Architecture d'Aujourd'hui, 1935), London: Faber and Faber, 1964, p. 139.

24 Le Corbusier, *The City of Tomorrow*, pp. 268–269.

25 Le Corbusier, *The City of Tomorrow* and Le Corbusier, *Towards a New Architecture*, (*Vers une architecture* Paris: G Crès et cie 1923), London: The Architectural Press, 1927, revised edition 1931, repr. 1989.

26 Tafuri, Manfredo, *Theories and History of Architecture*, New York: Granada, 1976, pp. 46–50.

27 Le Corbusier's thinking here is indebted to Nietzsche, see Nietzsche, Friedrich, *On the Advantage and Disavantage of History for Life* (*Vom Nutzen und Nachteil der Historie für das Leben 1874*), Peter Preuss, trans., Indianapolis and Cambridge: Hackett Publishing Company, 1980. For the impact of Nietzsche on Le Corbusier's thought, see Turner, Paul, *The Education of Le Corbusier: A Study of the Development of Le Corbusier's Thought 1900–1920*, New York and London: Garland, 1977, pp. 55–57.

28 Le Corbusier, *Towards a New Architecture*, p. 173.

29 Le Corbusier, *The Decorative Art of Today* (*L'Art décoratif d'aujourd'hui*, Paris: G Crès et cie, 1925), London: The Architectural Press, 1929, repr. 1987, p. 22.

30 Le Corbusier, *The Decorative Art of Today*, p. 21.

31 Le Corbusier, *The Decorative Art of Today*, p. 18.

32 Le Corbusier, *The Decorative Art of Today*, p. 16.

33 Le Corbusier, *The Decorative Art of Today*, p. 16.

34 Le Corbusier, *The Decorative Art of Today*, p. 16.

35 Le Corbusier and Pierre Jeanneret, *Œuvre Complète de 1938–1946*, Éditions d'Architecture, Erlenbach Zurich, 1946, p. 19. See also Le Corbusier and Pierre Jeanneret, *Œuvre Complète de 1910–1929*, Éditions Girsberger, Zurich, 1937, p. 193.

36 Le Corbusier, *Precisions* (*Précisions sur un état présent de l'architecture et de l'urbanisme*, Paris: G Crès et cie 1930), Cambridge, MA: MIT Press, 1991, p. 176.

37 Le Corbusier, *The City of Tomorrow*, p. 287.

38 Le Corbusier, *The Radiant City*, p. 103.

39 Le Corbusier, *Precisions* (*Précisions sur un état présent de l'architecture et de l'urbanisme*, Paris: G Crès et cie 1930), Cambridge, MA: MIT Press, 1991, p. 199.

40 Le Corbusier, *Precisions*, p. 199.

41 Le Corbusier, *Precisions*, p. 198.

42 Le Corbusier, *The City of Tomorrow*, pp. 176 and 243.

43 Le Corbusier, *The Radiant City*, p. 287.

44 Le Corbusier, *The Radiant City*, p. 138.

45 Le Corbusier, *The Radiant City*, p. 287.

46 Le Corbusier, *The Radiant City*, p. 168.

47 Le Corbusier, *The City of Tomorrow*, pp. 287–288.

48 Riegl, Alois, "The Modern Cult of Monuments: Its Character and its Origin", Kurt Forster and Diane Ghirardo trans., *Oppositions*, 25, 1982, p. 39.

49 Charles, Prince of Wales, *A Vision of Britain: A Personal View of Architecture*, London: Transworld Publishers, 1989.

50 Le Corbusier, *The City of Tomorrow*, p. 288.

PROXIMITY AND DISTANCE

The notion of a common heritage protected for the wellbeing of all by national and global institutions has become such an integrated part of our thinking that we often overlook its historical specificity. Acts that challenge this notion are met with shock and condemned on a broad front; the international outcry against the Taliban's destruction of the Buddhist statues in Afghanistan during 2001 is an example that illustrates this point. When the media in the beginning of 2001 started reporting about the Taliban destruction of museum collections and pre-Islamic Buddha-statues, Unesco issued several statements that strongly criticised the actions as "crimes against culture".[1] Despite widespread condemnation the giant Buddha-statues in the Bamiyan Valley were destroyed in a carefully staged media event that pointed to Taliban awareness of the significance of this destruction for the international community. In 2003 the whole Bamiyan Valley was assigned World Heritage status and simultaneously placed on Unesco's list for Heritage in Danger. Noticeably the Buddha Statues in the valley were not classified as World Heritage until they were destroyed and mutilated. Since then international support and investment has been offered to consolidate the area's status and to work for making it accessible for visitors as part of the network of global heritage sites distributed through the World Heritage List. Like the symbolically loaded destruction of the Bastille, discussed in the first chapter, the destruction of the Bamiyan Buddha's stands out as an extreme case showing how the opposition between preservation and destruction is preliminary and varying, shifting according to contexts, sites and audiences.

A crucial aim with this book has been to reflect on the historical formations that have informed such contemporary thinking around heritage. Architectural heritage might appear as immovable and durable in its presence, resistant both to display and to displacement. However as noted here—from *Musée des monuments français'* displaced fragment to Viollet-le-Duc's reconstructions, to John Ruskin's daguerreotypes of Venice and Le Corbusier's Plan Voisin—architectural objects have constituted material for a

Thomas Struth.
Rijksmuseum 1,
Amsterdam 1990.
Chromogenic print.

curatorial practice where buildings in both a real and imaginary sense are collected and displayed. The alteration of a building's context; the moving of an object from one site to another; re-naming and re-classification through legal frameworks such as listing and shifted ownership; re-framing through strategies of display and mediation; all these can be read as curatorial interventions that affect the value and meaning of the object for the beholder in critical ways. Conservation even when its aim is to preserve an object or a site in its current form without alteration or restoration, establishes a distance between the present existence of the object and its past. Classified as heritage, buildings turn into 'special' objects relocated into the realm of cultural history, a space that can be understood generically, if not always physically, as that of the museum.

In the discussion of the French Revolution's iconoclasm, the museum was identified as the specific space in which a modern notion of heritage emerged. Through physical dislocation and re-categorisation, the museum turned objects of veneration into historical objects to be rationally and aesthetically contemplated.

By the late nineteenth century legislation and institutions that were to control and care for a national patrimony were in place in most parts of Europe. These reinforcements were not without political implications and often reflected a strained relation between church and state. In the realm of conservation this struggle was played out over the issue of which institution was to be responsible for the restoration of religious buildings: who was to have the prerogative of interpretation? Were religious buildings to be inscribed in the national history as historical monuments controlled by the state or were they, as cult-buildings, the responsibility of the church? This was a crucial issue in the French Revolution's debate on vandalism and these issues also emerged in Viollet-le-Duc's theory of restoration. In both these cases it was argued that conservation was a means to estrange the objects from the cult; either re-framed or re-built they became historical objects to be judged within the realm of criticism. Conservation can therefore be understood as a form of secularisation of objects and buildings with an ultimate connection to the idea of the museum as a space of criticism. Incorporated into the history of the nation, as examples of the achievements of its people, religious buildings could no longer be understood as a part of God's presence on earth. As examples of specific building-periods they turned into representations, illustrating the development of the history of architecture. History then, replaced the cult.

The longing for a return to an original non-historicised relation to the object has haunted the discourse of heritage ever since. This longing conditions the field of conservation at large, expressed not least in a fixation with, and a repeated disappointment in the authentic. It inscribes the heritage object in a complex theme of proximity and distance, which runs throughout the history of conservation and finds its expression in various alternative spatial regimes. In John Ruskin's critique of conservation one can identify a melancholic desire to reinstate a relation to the object that was unmediated and in some way spaceless, lacking the distance necessary for 'History' to take place. Le Corbusier's double attitude to the museum as both a place of instruction and destruction also evokes a certain longing for authenticity that appears to be denied in the space of the museum. His aim to liberate the historical monuments from the forces of modern urbanity—speed, noise, congestion—through the means of destruction and to reframe them in an arcadian landscape, reveals a longing for a meeting with an authentic past. In Riegl's theory of a modern cult of monuments this meeting is the very hinge that opens the present to the past.

This yearning for closeness also directs the increasingly restless and expanding audience for heritage today. The heritage tourist appears to be driven by the perception that what is longed for is not to be found in the immediate surroundings; indeed the heritage industry feeds on the fact of distance and the promise of proximity. And yet, as anyone will discern who has travelled to experience treasures from the past at close hand, the restrictions installed in-situ as protection—restricted access, barriers, prohibition to touch or even document the object in question—re-enact the delays of travel itself. The longing to be close is denied by distance played out in space and time.

In this book the ocular bias of heritage, its dedication to the visual, has been seen as the key to understanding the potency of the monument in contemporary society. A key argument has been that perceived or real dangers move buildings into the realm of the visual where, understood in a wide sense as images, they become monumentalised. Strategies of conservation, from the consolidation of patina, to full reconstructions, can all be understood as scopic technologies that in an increasingly advanced manner administrate material stuff so that it returns to us as an image of the past. On an urban level the force of heritage is implicated in a set of visual desires and politics that are spatially conditioned. Integrated into a pervasive visual culture where images trigger desires and fantasies, the place-bound heritage monument acts as an agent in the marketing of cities and areas as desirable objects for cultural consumption in-situ. But also in a deeper and more political sense it has been suggested that cultures of conservation have effected, transformed, and re-enacted the relationship between man and objects (objects here understood in the widest sense to include everything from individual discreet articles of cultural patrimony in museums to cities and regions). The monument and its conservation has been understood primarily as a set of conflicting issues of representation, where notions of iconoclasm and idolatry are often conflated and interchanged.

POSTSCRIPT

In 2002 I travelled to the Val di Noto, in south-east Sicily, to visit the baroque cities of the region, then in the process of being inscribed onto Unesco's World Heritage List. Noto, the 'capital' of Sicilian Baroque, together with eight other urban Baroque environments, was nominated as an "outstanding testimony to the exuberant genius of late Baroque art and architecture".[2]

Two seismic events lay behind Val di Noto's qualification as a World Heritage Site. The first was a catastrophic earthquake in 1693. The earthquake destroyed large parts of the region and in the following century several towns in the Val di Noto area were totally rebuilt, either in-situ or relocated to new sites. This major disaster opened the possibility for rebuilding the cities according to urban baroque ideals prevalent at the time. The effort to create entire new urban realities after such a major catastrophe was, specifically in the first nomination of Val di Noto to Unesco, identified as an 'object' of conservation; the organisational capacity behind the re-construction was cited as one of the main criteria for the area's elevation to World Heritage status. The nomination also underlined the seismic risk in the area as a contributing qualification.

The nomination and inscription of Val di Noto on the World Heritage list illustrates on many levels the argument of this book, from the presence of danger and risk when an object is defined as a monument, to the expansion and widening of the monument as a category. In the nomination of Val de Noto it is intriguing that it is not the individual masterpieces of architecture or the urban configurations but the very process of creating this outstanding architecture that is suggested to constitute the 'historical monument' to be protected. This points to the widening of the monument as a category for conservation from discreet individual buildings, to environments, to building processes, and, in the end, even to the social process of commissioning and execution.

When I visited Noto the cathedral was covered by scaffolding and under restoration. To diminish the effect of a missing part in the urban baroque composition surrounding the church, a photograph of its front facade, printed 1:1 in full colour, had been hung in front of the scaffolding. With the on-going world heritage nomination, the pressure of making the city visitable was evident at the time. Together with a group of tourists, who had travelled as I had for hours to reach this destination, I peered somewhat in vain at the enormous full-sized image slowly moving in the wind, feeling a familiar overwhelming disappointment of not 'meeting' the main protagonist of my tour.

The full sized image at Noto can exemplify a fundamental condition of the heritage monument—the issue of representation and mimesis. The photographic veil hid effectively the danger and ruination created by the second event that had triggered Val di Noto's world heritage listing. During the evening of 13 March 1996 the central nave and part of the dome of the cathedral dramatically collapsed as a result of an earthquake six years earlier, which had aggravated already existing structural problems in the church. After three years of extensive archaeological excavation and investigation, aimed at identifying the original position of the stones within the cathedral's structure in order to analyse the structural reason for the collapse, the rebuilding began in 1999. The church opened in 2007; re-constructed using traditional building methods and materials. In February 2011 the church was re-consecrated.[3]

At the time of my visit in 2002 the area of the cathedral behind the screen looked more like a site of demolition than of restoration. To consolidate the structure further parts of the church had to be demolished and the removal of the rubble was an operation of impressive scale. And yet when looking at the large-scale photograph I was reassured, despite the fact that there was not much left behind the front facade at the time, that something very like the photograph would soon be there. The photograph in Noto contained an indexical promise I could not resist. It showed a 'thereness' of something not there, suggesting the possibility of retrieval. Yet a seed of suspicion towards the object returning on the other side of the veil is implicated in this promise. The reconstruction of Noto Cathedral aims on one level to merge the image of the cathedral with the materiality that supports that image—to make them one and the same. The advancing of the technology of conservation, the increased knowledge of material and building traditions, can be understood in relation to this. Resurrected, the re-constructed monument will be judged on how well it resembles and even behaves like itself (the restoration at Noto included an effort to research and find local stone with the same behavioural properties as the original). Here issues of identity and likeness go beyond the surface and yet are still conditioned by ocular desires. Conservation becomes the action of making the historical monument support its representation— to make its object-hood merge with its image.

NOTES

1 *See: Official Records*, A/55/PV.94 United Nations, General Assembly, plenary meeting Friday, 9 March 2001, 10 am, New York.

2 The Val di Noto 'collection' of urban environments, spread over an extensive area, was first nominated in 22 June 2000 with a revised nomination in 11 January 2002 to finally become selected in August 2002. See further: Evaluation NOTO (ITALY) NO1224REV: see: whc. unesco.org/archive/advisory_body_evaluation/1024rev. pdf (downloaded 2011.11.01) and decision: see: http:// whc.unesco.org/archive/decrec02.htm#dec23-17 (downloaded 2011.11.01)

3 This was not the first time Noto Cathedral had gone through such a process. Built in different phases from 1764, the cathedral was opened to worshippers in 1776 but only four years later its dome collapsed and was re-built. In 1848 after yet another earthquake this cycle of collapse and rebuilding was repeated. A new dome designed by the engineer Cascone in a novel technique was completed in 1872. During the 1950s the Cathedral was extensively restored and re-built, the lower part being covered by new rendering and a new concrete roof completed in 1960. Thus the Cathedral had then been more or less constantly under reconstruction and rebuilding since its inauguration. This monument, rather than a static object, was an on-going movement of stones in a processual repetition framed by re-constructions and re-buildings. See further "The Difficult Choice of Materials for the Reconstruction of the Cathedral of Noto" Binda Luiga et al, in *Fracture and Failure of Natural Building Stones*, Stavros K Kourkoulis eds., Dordrecht: Springer, 2006, pp.185–200.

BIBLIOGRAPHY

Studies in Cultural Studies, Linköping University Electronic Press.

———, "The Cult of Age", *Future Anterior, Journal of Historic Preservation, History Theory and Criticism*, Columbia University, May 2004.

———, "The Fragile Monument: On Riegl's Modern Cult of Monuments." (theorising) *History in Architecture, Proceedings of the Nordic Journal of Architectural Research*, Elizabeth Tostrup and Christian Hermansen, eds., Oslo, 2003.

———, "The Metaphor for the New", *Nordic Journal of Architectural Research*, No. 2, 1999, pp. 57–62.

———, "The Phenomena of Restoration", *Magasin för Modern Arkitektur*, No. 18, 1997, pp. 14–15.

———, "Restoration and Modernity: The Enigma of the Old in the Era of The New", *Nordic Journal of Architectural Research*, No. 2, 2002, pp. 69–71.

———, "Restoration in the Machine Age: Themes of Conservation in Le Corbusier's Plan Voisin", *AA Files*, Vol. 38, 1999, pp. 10–22.

———, "Unintentional Monuments", *Index Art Magazine*, No. 3–4, 1997, pp. 60–1/100–101.

Ashworth, GJ, Brian Graham, et al., *Pluralising Past, Heritage Identity and and Place in Multicultural Societies*, London and Ann Arbor, MI: Pluto Press, 2007.

Bacher, Ernst, *Kunstwerk oder Denkmal? Alois Riegls Schriften zur Denkmalpflege*, Wien, Köln, Weimar: Böhlau Verlag, 1995.

Baczko, Bronislaw, "Vandalism", *A Critical Dictionary of the French Revolution*, François Furet and Mona Ozouf eds., Cambridge, MA: Harvard University Press, 1989.

Banham, Reyner, *Theory and Design in the First Machine Age*, London: Architectural Press, 1960.

Bann, Stephen, *The Clothing of Clio: A Study of the Representation of History in Nineteenth-Century Britain and France*, Cambridge: Cambridge University Press, 1984.

Barthes, Roland, *Camera Lucida: Reflections on Photography*, Richard Howard trans., New York: Hill and Wang, 1981.

Batchen, Geoffrey, *Burning with Desire: The Conception of Photography*, Cambridge, MA: MIT Press, 1997.
Bek, Lise, and Henrik Oxvig, eds., *Rumanalyser*, Århus: Fonden til udgivelse af Arkitekturtidsskrift B, 1997.

Adorno, Theodor W, "Valéry, Proust Museum", Samuel Weber and Shierry Weber trans., *Prisms*, (Prismen: Kulturkritik und Gesellschaft, Suhrkamp, Berlin, 1955), Camridge, MA: MIT Press, 1981.

Allais, Lucia, "Will To War; Will To Art; Cultural Internationalism and the Modernist Aesthetics of Monuments", PhD dissertation, MIT, 2008.

Anstey, Tim, Kaja Grillner and Rolf Huges eds, *Architecture and Authorship*, London: Black Dog Publishing, 2007.

Appadurai, Arjun, *Modernity at Large*, Minneapolis: University of Minnesota Press, (1996) 2010.

Arrhenius, Thordis, "Preservation and Protest, Counterculture and Heritage in 1970's Sweden", *Future Anterior, Journal of Historic Preservation, History Theory and Criticism*, Vol. VII 2, 2010.

———, "The Vernacular On Display", *Swedish Modernism, Architecture, Consumption, and the Welfare State*, London: Black Dog Publishing, 2010.

———, "The pleasure of the Surface" *Jorge Otero-Pailos: The Ethics of Dust*, Eva Ebersberger and Daniela Zyman eds., Köln: Verlag der Buchhandlung Walther König, 2009

———, "Meaning in Western Architecture, Notes on the Monument", *An Eye for Place: Christian Norberg-Schulz: Architect, Teacher and Historian*, Oslo: Pax, 2008.

———, "Bevarandets rum", *Agora: journal for metafysisk spekulasjon*, Oslo, 2006.

———, "Ruskin's Daguerreotypes in Venice", Proceedings of the Nordic Conference for Advanced

Benjamin, Walter, "Rigorous Study of Art", Thomas Y Levin trans., *October*, Vol. 47, 1988, pp. 84–90.

Bennett, Tony, *The Birth of the Museum: History, Theory, Politics*, London: Routledge, 1995.

Benton, Tim, ed., *Understanding Heritage and Memory*, Manchester: Manchester University Press, 2010.

———, *The Villas of Le Corbusier 1920–1930*, New Haven: Yale University Press, 1987.

Bergdoll, Barry, "The Dictionnaire raisonné of Viollet-le-Duc", *The Foundations of Architecture: Selections from the 'Dictionnaire raisonné'*, New York: Brazillier, 1990.

———, "The Legacy of Viollet-le-Duc's Drawings", *Architectural Record*, Vol. 169, No. 11, 1981, pp. 66–67.

———, "A Matter of Time: Architects and Photographers in Second Empire France", *The Photographs of Édouard Baldus*, Malcolm Daniel, ed., New York: The Metropolitan Museum of Art, 1994.

Bevan, Robert, *The Destruction of Memory*, London: Reaktion Books, 2006.

Binda, Luiga, et al, "The Difficult Choice of Materials for the Reconstruction of the Cathedral of Noto", *Fracture and Failure of Natural Building Stones*, Stavros K Kourkoulis ed., Dordrecht: Springer, 2006, pp.185–200.

Binstock, Benjamin, "Postscript: Alois Riegl in the Presence of 'The Nightwatch'", *October*, Vol. 74, Fall, 1995, pp. 36–44.

Boudon, Françoise, "Le réel et l'imaginaire chez Viollet-le-Duc: les figures du Dictionnaire de l'architecture", *Revue de l'art*, No. 58/59, 1983, pp. 95–114.

Bradley, John Lewis, ed., *Ruskin's Letters from Venice, 1851–1852*, New Haven: Yale University Press, 1955.

Bressani, Martin, "The Life of Stones: Viollet-le-Duc's Physiology of Architecture", *ANY: Architecture New York*, No. 14, 1996, pp. 23–27.

Brooks, Allen H, ed., *Le Corbusier: Essays*, Princeton, NJ: Princeton University Press, 1987.

Brown, Gerard Baldwin, "The Care of Ancient Monuments: An account of the legislative and other measures adopted in European Countries for protecting ancient monuments and objects and scenes of natural beauty, and for preserving the aspect of historical cities", (1905), Cambridge: Cambridge University Press, 2010.

Burns, Karen, "Topographies of Tourism: "Documentary" Photography and "The Stones of Venice"", *Assemblage*, No. 32, 1997, pp. 22–44.

Cacciari, Massimo, Architecture and Nihilism: *On the Philosophy of Modern Architecture*, Stephen Sartarelli trans., New Haven, CT.: Yale University Press, 1993.

Charles, Prince of Wales, *A Vision of Britain: A Personal View of Architecture*, London: Transworld Publishers, 1989.

Choay, Françoise, *L'allégorie du patrimoine*, Paris: Seuil, 1992.

———, "Riegl, Freud et les monuments historiques: pour une approche sociétale de la préservation", *World Art, Themes of Unity in Diversity*, Irving Lavin, ed., University Park, Pennsylvania: Pennsylvania State University Press, 1986.

Christ, Yvan, *L'Age d'or de la Photographie*, Paris: Vincent, Fréal et Cie, 1965.

Clegg, Jeanne, and Paul Tucker, *Ruskin and Tuscany*, London: Ruskin Gallery in Sheffield, Collection of the Guild of St George in association with Lund Humphries, 1993.

Cobban, Alfred, *A History of Modern France, 1715–1799*, London: Penguin/Harmondsworth, 1983.

Colomina, Beatriz, *Privacy and Publicity: Modern Architecture as Mass Media*, Cambridge, MA: MIT Press, 1994.

Colquhoun, Alan, *Modernity and the Classical Tradition: Architectural Essays 1980–1987*, Cambridge, MA: MIT Press, 1989.

Convention Concerning the Protection of the World Cultural and Natural Heritage: Adopted by the General Conference at Its Seventeenth Session, Paris, 16 November 1972, Paris: Unesco, 1972.

Cormack, Patrick, *Heritage in Danger*, London: New English Library, 1976.

Costantini, Paolo, and Italo Zannier, eds., *I Dagherrotipi Della Collezione Ruskin*, Firenze: Alinari, 1986.

Courajod, Louis, *Alexandre Lenoir et le Musée des Monuments Français*, Paris: Libraire Honoré Champion, 1878–1886.

Cousins, Mark, "Chronography", *Random Walk*, Christian Nicolas and Eyal Weizman, eds., London: Architectural Association, 1998.

———, "The Ugly", *Index Art Magazine*, No. 3–4, 1996, pp. 79–85/124–130.

Cousins, Mark, and Athar Hussain, *Michel Foucault*, London: Macmillan, 1984.

Crary, Jonathan, *Techniques of the Observer: On Vision and Modernity in the Nineteenth Century*, Cambridge, MA.: MIT Press, 1990.

Crimp, Douglas, *On the Museum's Ruins*, Cambridge, MA: MIT Press, 1993.

Cruickshank, Dan, and Colin Amery, *The Rape of Britain*, London: Paul Elek, 1975.

Curtis, William JR, *Le Corbusier: Ideas and Forms*, Oxford: Phaidon, 1986.

Daguerre, Louis Jacques Mandes, "Daguerreotype", *Classic Essays on Photography*, Alan Trachtenberg, ed., New Haven: Leete's Island Books, 1980.

Damisch, Hubert, *The Origin of Perspective*, Cambridge, MA: MIT Press, 1994.

Denslagen, Wim, *Architectural Restoration in Western Europe: Controversy and Continuity*, Amsterdam: Architectura & Natura Press, 1994.

Déotte, Jean–Louis, "Rome, the Archetypal Museum and the Louvre, the Negation of Division", *Art in Museums*, Susan Pearce, ed., London: Athlone Press, 1995.

Despois, Eugène, *Le vandalisme révolutionnaire*, Paris: Germer Baillière, 1848.

Doyle, William, *The Oxford History of the French Revolution*, Oxford: Clarendon Press, 1989.

Durant, Stuart, "'Nulla Dies sine Linea': Viollet-le-Duc's Drawings", *Eugène Emmanuel Viollet-le-Duc, 1814–79*, London: Academy Editions, 1980.

Edman, Victor, *En Svensk Restaureringstradition, tre arkitekter gestaltar 1900-talets historiesyn*, Stockholm: Byggförlaget, 1999.

Elsner, Jas, "The Birth of Late Antiquity: Riegl and Strzygowski in 1901", *Journal of the Association of Art History*, Vol. 25, No. 3, June, 2002.

Elwall, Robert, *Photography Takes Command: The Camera and British Architecture 1890-39*, London: Heinz Gallery, 1994.

Etlin, Richard A., *Frank Lloyd Wright and Le Corbusier: The Romantic Legacy*, Manchester: Manchester University Press, 1994.

———, *Symbolic Space : French Enlightenment Architecture and Its Legacy*, Chicago: University of Chicago Press, 1994.

Evenson, Norma, *Le Corbusier : The Machine and the Grand Design*, London: Studio Vista, 1974.

Fairclought, Graham, Rodney Harrison, et al., eds., *The Heritage Reader*, London and New York: Routledge, 2008.

Fawcett, Jane, ed., *The Future of the Past: Attitudes to Conservation 1174–1974*, London: Thames & Hudson, 1976.

Fishman, Robert, *Urban Utopias in the Twentieth Century: Ebenezer Howard, Frank Lloyd Wright and Le Corbusier*, New York: Basic Books, 1977.

Forster, Kurt W., "Monument/Memory and the Mortality of Architecture", *Oppositions*, No. 25, fall, 1982, pp. 2–18.

Foucault, Michel, *The Order of Things. An Archaeology of the Human Sciences*, New York: Random House, Inc., 1973.

Freedberg, David, *Iconoclasts and Their Motives*, Maarssen: Gary Schwartz, 1985.

———, *The Power of Images: Studies in the History and Theory of Response*, Chicago: University of Chicago Press, 1989.

Frisby, David, *Fragments of Modernity: Theories of Modernity in the Work of Simmel, Kracauer and Benjamin*, Cambridge: Polity Press, 1985.

Furet, François, *Interpreting the French Revolution*, Cambridge: Cambridge University Press, 1988.

———, *Revolutionary France 1770-1880*, Oxford: Blackwell, 1992.

Furet, François, and Mona Ozouf, *A Critical Dictionary of the French Revolution*, Cambridge, MA: Belknap Press of Harvard University Press, 1989.

Gamboni, Dario, *The Destruction of Art: Iconoclasm and Vandalism since the French Revolution*, London: Reaktion Books, 1997.

Giedion, Sigfried, *Mechanization Takes Command: A Contribution to Anonymous History*, New York: Norton, 1948.

———, Space, *Time and Architecture; The Growth of a New Tradition*, Cambridge, MA: Harvard University Press, 1966.

Glacken, Clarence J, *Traces on the Rhodian Shore: Nature and Culture in Western Thought from Ancient Times to the End of the Eighteenth Century*, Berkeley, CA.: University of California Press, 1967.

Gombrich, Ernst, *Art and Illusion: A Study in Psychology of Pictorial Representation*, Princeton, NJ: Princeton University Press, 1960.

Greene, Christopher, "Alexandre Lenoire and the Musée des Monuments Français during the French Revolution", *French Historical Studies*, Vol. XII, No. 2, fall, 1981, pp. 200–222.

Grégoire, Abbé Henri, "Instruction publique—Rapport sur les destructions opérées par le vandalisme et sur les moyens de le réprimer", Paris, 1794.

———, *Mémoires*, H Carnot, ed., Paris: Ambroise Dupont, 1837.

———, "Second rapport sur le vandalisme", Paris, 1794.

———, "Troisième rapport sur le vandalisme", Paris, 1795.

Gubser, Michael, *Time's Visible Surface: Alois Riegl and the Discourse on History and Temporality in Fin-de-Siecle Vienna*, Detroit: Wayne State University Press, 2006.

Guillaume Legrand, Jacques, *Essai sur l'histoire générale de l'architecture*, Paris 1809.

Hanson, Brian, "Carrying off the Grand Canal: Ruskin's Architectural Drawings and the Daguerreotype", *The Architectural Review*, No. Feb., 1981, pp. 104–109.

Harvey, Michael, "Ruskin and Photography", *The Oxford Art Journal*, Vol. 7, No. 2, 1985, pp. 25–33.

Haslam, Ray, "'For the Sake of the Subject': Ruskin and the Tradition of Architectural Illustration", *The Lamp of Memory, Ruskin, Tradition and Architecture*, Michael Wheeler and Nigel Whiteley, eds., Manchester: Manchester University Press, 1992.
Hegel, GWF, *Aesthetics*, TM Knox trans., Oxford: Oxford University Press, 1975.

Herman, Daniel, "Destructions et vandalisme pendant la Révolution Française", *Annales ESC*, Vol. 33, 1978, pp. 703–705.

Herscher, Andrew, *Violence Taking Place*, Standford: Standford University Press, 2010.

Hewison, Robert, *The Heritage Industry: Britain in a Climate of Decline*, London: Methuen, 1987.

———, *Ruskin on Venice*, New Haven and London: Yale University Press, 2009.

Hunt, Lynn, *Politics, Culture, and Class in the French Revolution*, Berkeley: University of California Press, 1984.

Huyssen, Andreas, "Monument and Memory in a Postmodern Age", *Yale Journal of Criticism*, Vol. 6, No. 2, 1993.

Idzerda, Stanley J, "Iconoclasm during the French Revolution", *American Historical Review*, Vol. 60, No. 1, 1954, pp. 13–26.

Imbert, Dorothée, *The Modernist Garden in France*, New Haven: Yale University Press, 1993.

Impey, Oliver, and Arthur MacGregor, eds., *The Origins of Museums: The Cabinet of Curiosities in Sixteenth- and Seventeenth-Century Europe*, Oxford: Clarendon Press, 1985.

Iversen, Margaret, *Alois Riegl: Art History and Theory*, Cambridge, MA: MIT Press, 1993.

Janson, Sverker, *Kulturvård och Samhällsbildning*, Stockholm: Nordiska Museet, 1974.

Jarzombek, Mark, "De-Scribing the Language of Looking: Wölfflin and the History of Aesthetic Experientialism", *Assemblage*, Vol. 23, 1994, pp. 28–69.

———, *The Psychologizing of Modernity: Art, Architecture, History*, Cambridge: Cambridge University Press, 2000.

———, "Recognizing Ruskin: Modern Painters and the Refraction of Self", *Assemblage*, Vol. 32, 1997, pp. 70–87.

———, *Urban Heterology, Dresden and the Dialectics of Post-traumatic History*, Lund: School of Architecture, Lund University, 2001.

Jay, Martin, *Downcast Eyes: The Denigration of Vision in Twentieth-Century French Thought*, Berkeley, CA: University of California Press, 1993.

Jokilehto, Jukka, *A History of Architectural Conservation*, Oxford: Butterworth-Heinemann, 1999.

Jonsson, Marita, *Monumentvårdens begynnelse: Restaureringar och friläggning av antika monument i Rom 1800–1830*, Stockholm: Almquist&Wiksell International, 1976.

Kant, Immanuel, *The Critique of Pure Reason*, N Kemp Smith trans., London: Macmillan, 1929.

Kraucauer, Siegfried, "Photography", Thomas Y Levin trans., *Critical Inquiry*, Vol. 19, 1993, pp. 424–425.

Kulturminnesvård: betänkande 1965 års musei- och utställningssakkunniga (MUS 65), Stockholm: Liber förlag, 1972.

Kåring, Göran, "När medeltidens sol gått ned", Stockholm: Kungl. Vitterhets Historie och Antikvitets Akademien, 1992.

Lacan, Jacques, *Écrits: A Selection*, Alan Sheridan trans., London: Routledge, 1997.

———, *The Four Fundamental Concepts of Psycho-analysis*, Alan Sheridan trans., London: Penguin Books, 1994.

Lavin, Sylvia, *Quatremère De Quincy and the Invention of a Modern Language of Architecture*, Cambridge, MA: MIT Press, 1992.

Le Corbusier, *L'Art décoratif d'aujourd'hui*, (Translated as *The Decorative Art of Today*, The Architectural Press, London, 1929, repr. 1987.), Paris: G Crès et cie, 1925.

———, *La Ville Radieuse*, (Translated as *The Radiant City*, Faber and Faber, London, 1964.), Paris: Éditions de l'Architecture d'Aujourd'hui, 1935.

———, *Précisions sur un état présent de l'architecture et de l'urbanisme*, (Translated as *Precisions*, MIT Press, Cambridge, MA, 1991.), Paris: G Crès et cie, 1930.

———, *Quand les cathédrales étaient blanches*, (Translated as *When the Cathedrals Were White*, Reynal and Hitchcock, New York, 1942.), Paris: Plon, 1937.

———, *Urbanisme*, (Translated as *The City of Tomorrow*, The Architectural Press, London, 1929, repr. 1987.), Paris: Crès et cie, 1925.

———, *Vers une architecture*, (Translated as *Towards a New Architecture*, The Architectural Press, London 1927, revised edition 1931, repr. 1989), Paris: Crès et cie, 1923.

Le Corbusier, and Pierre Jeanneret, *Œuvre complète de 1910–1929*, Zurich: Éditions Girsberger, 1937.

———, *Œuvre complète de 1938–1946*, Erlenbach-Zurich: Éditions d'Architecture, 1946.

Lefebvre, Georges, *La France sous le Directoire, 1795-1799*, Paris: Éditions Sociales, 1977.

Lenoire, Alexandre, *Description historique et chronologique des monumens de sculptures renuis au Musée des monumens français*, Paris: Musée des monumens français, 1803.

Levin, Thomas Y, "Benjamin and the Theory of Art History. An Introduction to the 'Rigorous Study of Art'", *October*, Vol. 47, 1988, pp. 77–83.

Lévy-Leboyer, Claude, ed., *Vandalism: Behaviour and Motivations*, Amsterdam: North Holland, 1984.

Lowenthal, David, *The Past Is a Foreign Country*, Cambridge: Cambridge University Press, 1985.

Malcolm, Daniel, ed., *The Photographs of Édouard Baldus*, New York: The Metropolitan Museum of Art, 1994.

Mallgrave, Harry Francis, ed., *Empathy, Form, and Space: Problems in German Aesthetics, 1873–1893*, Santa Monica, CA: Getty Center for the History of Art and the Humanities, 1994.

Marot, Pierre, "L'abbé Grégoire et la vandalisme révolutionaire", *Revue de l'Art*, Vol. 49, 1980, pp. 36–39.

Mattson, Helena, "Arkitektur och konsumption: Reyner Banham och utbytbarhetens estetik", Stockholm: School of Architecture Stockholm, Royal Institute of Technology, 2003.

———, "Designing the Reasonable Consumer. Standardisation and Personalisation in Swedish Functionalism", *Swedish Modernism, Architecture Consumption and the Welfare State*, Helena Mattson and Sven-Olov Wallenstein, eds., London: Black Dog Publishing, 2010.

Mattsson, Helena, and Sven-Olov Wallenstein, eds., *Swedish Modernism, Architecture Consumption and the Welfare State*, London: Black Dog Publishing, 2010.

McCauley, Elizabeth Anne, *Industrial Madness: Commercial Photography in Paris, 1848–1871*, New Haven, CT: Yale University Press, 1994.

Merleau-Ponty, Maurice, *The Visible and the Invisible*, Alphonso Lingis trans., Claude Lefort, ed., Evanston, IL: Northwestern University Press, 1968.

Millin, Aubin Louis, *Antiquités nationales ou Recueil de monumens pour servir à l'histoire générale et particulière de l'Empire français*, 6 Vols., Paris, 1790–1795.

Prospectus presenting *Antiquités nationales ou Recueil de monumens*, Paris, 1790. Source: British Library, French Tracts on Science, BL: 936.f.9 (28).

Moos, Stanislaus von, *Le Corbusier: Elements of a Synthesis*, Cambridge, MA: MIT Press, 1979.

———, "Le Corbusier: The Monument and the Metropolis", *Columbia Documents of Architecture and Theory*, Vol. 3, 1993.

Munch, Anders V, *Den stilløse stil—Adolf Loos*, København: Kunstakademiets Arkitekskoles Forlag, 2002.

Munoz Vinas, Salvador, *Contemporary Theory of Conservation*, London: Elsevier Butterworth-Heinemann, 2005.

Murphy, Kevin D, *Memory and Modernity: Viollet-Le-Duc at Vézelay*, University Park, PA: Pennsylvania State University Press, 2000.

Mårtelius, Johan, *Göra arkitekturen historisk: om 1800-talets arkitekturtänkande och IG Clasons Nordiska museum*, Stockholm: Arkitekturmuseet, 1987.

———, "Hotet mot Paris", *Le Corbusier och Stockholm*, Stockholm: Arkitekturmuseet, 1987.

Nietzsche, Fredrich, *On the Advantages and Disadvantages of History for Life*, Peter Preuss trans., Indianapolis, Cambridge: Hackett Publishing Company, 1980.

Nochlin, Linda, *The Body in Pieces: The Fragment as a Metaphor of Modernity*, London: Thames & Hudson, 1994.

Nora, Pierre, "Between Memory and History", (in *Les Lieux de Mémoire*, Vol. I, ed. Pierre Nora, Edition Gallimard, Paris 1984), Marc Roudebush trans., *Representations*, Vol. 26, spring, 1989, pp. 7–25.

O'Conell, Lauren, M, "Viollet-le-Duc on Drawing, Photography and the 'Space Outside the Frame'", *History of Photography*, Vol. 22, No. 2, summer, 1998, pp. 139–145.

Olin, Margaret, "The Cult of Monuments as a State Religion in late 19th Century Austria", *Wiener Jahrbuch für Kunstgeschichte*, 1985.

———, *Forms of Representation in Alois Riegl's Theory of Art*, University Park, PA: Pennsylvania State University Press, 1992.

Ozouf, Mona, *Festivals and the French Revolution*, Cambridge, MA, and London: Harvard University Press, 1988.

Panofsky, Erwin, *Meaning in the Visual Arts: Papers in and on Art History*, Garden City, NY: Doubleday, 1955.

Pendlebury, John, *Conservation in the Age of Consensus*, London and New York: Routledge, 2009.

Pettersson, Richard, *Den Svenska kulturmiljöns värdegrunder*, Umeå: Umeå University, 2003.

———, *Fädernesland och Framtidsland, Sigurd Curman och Kulturminnesvården Etablering*, Umeå: Umeå University, 2001.

Pevsner, Nikolaus, *Ruskin and Viollet-Le-Duc: Englishness and Frenchness in the Appreciation of Gothic Architecture*, London: Thames & Hudson, 1969.

———, "Scrape and anti-scrape", *The Future of the Past. Attitudes to Conservation 1174–1974*, Jane Fawcett, ed., London: Thames & Hudson, 1976.

Podro, Michael, *The Critical Historians of Art*, New Haven, CT: Yale University Press, 1982.

———, *The Manifold in Perception: Theories of Art from Kant to Hildebrand*, Oxford: Clarendon, 1972.

Pommier, Edouard, "Discourse iconoclaste, discourse culturel, discourse national. 1790–1794", *Révolution Française et "Vandalisme" Revolutionnaire*, Paris: Universitas, 1992.

———, "La théorie des arts", *Aux armes et aux arts, Les arts de la Revolution 1789–1799*, Philippe Bordes and Régis Michel, eds., Paris: Éditions Adam Biro, 1988.

———, ed., *Lettres à Miranda sur les déplacements de monuments de l'art de Italie par Quatremère de Quincy*, Paris: Éditions Macula, 1989.

Poulot, Dominique, "Alexandre Lenoir et les musées des monuments français", *Les Lieux de Mémoire*, II, Pierre Nora, ed., Paris: Éditions Gallimard, 1992.

———, *Musée, nation, patrimoine 1789–1815*, Paris: Éditions Gallimard, 1997.

———, "Revolutionary 'Vandalism' and the Birth of the Museum: The Effects of a Representation of Modern Cultural Terror", *Art in Museums*, Susan Pearce, ed., London: Athlone Press, 1995.

"Procès-verbaux du Comité d'instruction publique de l'Assemblée Législative", Collection des Documents Inédits sur l'histoire de France, published and annotated with a commentary by MJ Guillaume, Paris: Librairie Hachette et Cie, 1889.

Pugin, Augustus Welby, *Contrast: or, a Parallel between the Noble Edifices of the Fourteenth and Fifteenth centuries, and Similar Buildings of the Present day; Showing the Present Decay of Taste*, London: printed and published by the author, 1836.

Pächt, Otto, "Art Historians and Art Critics—VI: Alois Riegl", *Burlington Magazine*, Vol. 105, 1963, pp. 188–193.

Quatremère de Quincy, *Antoine Chrysotôme, Considérations morales sur la destination des ouvrages de l'art*, Paris: repr. Fayard, 1989.

———, "Dictionnaire d'architecture", *Encyclopédie méthodique*, Panckoucke ed., Paris, 3 Vols., 1788–1825.

Réau, Louis, *Histoire du vandalisme. Les monuments détruits de l'art français*, (1958, augmented edition ed. Michel Fleury and Guy-Michel Leproux), Paris: Robert Laffont réédition, 1994.

Reiff, DD, "Viollet-le-Duc and Historical Restoration: The West Portal of Notre-Dame", *Journal of Architectural Historians*, Vol. 30, No. 1, March, 1971, pp. 17–30.

Revel, Jacques, and Lynn Hunt, eds., *Histories: French Constructions of the Past, Post-war French Thought*, New York: The New Press, 1995.

Reynolds, Diana Graham, "Alois Riegl and the Politics of Art History: Intellectual Traditions and Austrian Identity in Fin de Siècle Vienna", Ann Arbor: University of California at San Diego, 1997.

Rice, Shelley, *Parisian views*, Cambridge, MA: MIT Press, 1997.

Riegl, Alois, "Das Riesenthor zu St. Stephan", (Neue Freie Presse, February 1902), in Ernst Bacher, *Kunstwerk oder Denkmal? Alois Riegls Schriften zur Denkmalpflege*, Wien, Köln and Weimar: Böhlau Verlag, 1995, pp. 147–156.

———, "Den Moderne Minnesmerkekulturens Vesen og Tilblivelse", ("Der Moderne Denkmalkultus. Sein Wesen und Seine Entstehung", 1903), Sverre Dahl trans., Agora, No. 3, 2006, pp. 203–216.

———, *The Group Portraiture of Holland*, (Das holländische Gruppenporträt, Jahrbuch des allerhöchsten Kaiserhauses 23, 1902), Evelyn M Kain and David Britt trans., Los Angeles: Getty Research Institute for the History of Art and the Humanities, 1999.

———, *Late Roman Art Industry*, (Die spätrömische Kunstindustrie nach den Funden in Österreich-Ungarn, Vienna: I Teil, K k Hof-und Staatsdruckerei, 1901), Rolf Winkes trans., Rome: Bretschneider, 1985.

———, "The Modern Cult of Monuments: Its Character and Its Origin", (Der moderne Denkmalkultus. Sein Wesen und seine Entstehung, Vienna 1903, republished in Konservieren, nicht restaurieren. Streitschriften zur Denkmalpflege um 1900, Braunschweig: Bauwelt Fundamente, Friedr. Vieweg & Sohn, 1988), Kurt Forster and Diane Ghirardo trans., *Oppositions*, Vol. 25, 1982, pp. 21–51. French translation: *Le Culte moderne des monuments, Son essence et sa genèse*, Daniel Wieczorek trans., Paris: Seuil, 1984.

———, "Neue Strömungen", (1905), in Bacher Ernst, *Kunstwerk oder Denkmal? Alois Riegls Schriften zur Denkmalpflege*, Wien, Köln and Weimar: Böhlau Verlag, 1995.

———, *The origins of Baroque art in Rome*, (Entstehung der Barockkunst in Rom, Vienna 1908), Andrew Hopkins and Arnold Witte eds. and trans., Los Angeles: Getty Research Institute, 2010.

———, *Problems of Style: Foundations for a History of Ornament*, (Stilfragen, Siemens, Berlin 1893), Evelyn Kain trans., Princeton and New York: Princeton University Press, 1992.

Rossi, Aldo, *The Architecture of the City*, Diane Ghirardo and Joan Ockman trans., Cambridge MA, and London: MIT Press, 1989.

Rowe, Colin, and Fred Koetter, *Collage City*, Cambridge, MA: MIT Press, 1973.

Ruskin, John, "The Complete Works of John Ruskin", ET Cook and Alexander Wedderburn eds., London: George Allan, 39 Vols., 1903–1912.

———, *Examples of the Architecture of Venice, Sketched and Drawn to Measurement from the Edifices, Sixteen Plates with Descriptions*, London: Smith, Elder & Co., 1851.

———, *The Seven Lamps of Architecture*, Kent: George Allan, 1880.

Rücker, Frédéric, *Les Origines de la conservation des monuments historiques en France, 1790–1830*, Paris: Jouve & Cie, 1913.

Rykwert, Joseph, *On Adam's House in Paradise: The Idea of the Primitive Hut in Architectural History*, New York: Museum of Modern Art, 1972.

Samuel, Raphael, *Theaters of Memory*, London: Verso, 1994.

Scarrocchia, Sandro, *Alois Riegl: teoria e prassi della conservazione dei monumenti*, Bologna: Clueb, 1995.

Schama, Simon, *Citizens: A Chronicle of the French Revolution*, New York: Alfred A Knopf : Distributed by Random House, 1989.

Schorske, Carl E, *Fin-de-Siècle Vienna, Politic and Culture*, New York: repub. Random House, 1981.

Semper, Gottfried, *Der Stil in den technischen und tectonishen Künsten oder praktische Aesthetik*, Frankfurt: 1860, 1863.

———, *The Four Elements of Architecture and Other Writings*, and introduction by Harry F Mallgrave trans., Cambridge: Cambridge University Press, 1989.

Sennett, Richard, *The Conscience of the Eye: The Design and Social Life of Cities*, London: Faber and Faber, 1990.

Seroux d'Agincourt, Jean Baptiste, *Histoire de l'art par les monuments*, Paris: Treuttel et Würtz, 1823.

Shapiro, Harold L, ed., *Ruskin in Italy: Letters to his Parents*, 1845, Oxford: Clarendon, 1972.

Sherman, Daniel J, *Worthy Monuments, Art Museums and Politics of Culture in Nineteenth-century France*, Cambridge MA: Harvard University Press, 1989.

Smith, Laurajane, *Archeological Theory and the Politics of Cultural Heritage*, London: Routledge, 2004.

———, *Intangible Heritage*, London and New York: Routledge, 2009.

———, *Uses of Heritage*, London and New York: Routledge, 2006.

Smith, Lindsay, *Victorian Photography, Painting and Poetry: The Enigma of Visibility in Ruskin, Morris and the Pre-Raphaelites*, Cambridge: Cambridge University Press, 1995.

Stanley Price, NP, M Kirby Talley, et al., eds., *Historical and Philosophical Issues in the Conservation of Cultural Heritage*, Los Angeles, CA: Getty Conservation

Stewart, Susan, *On Longing: Narratives of the Miniature, the Gigantic, the Souvenir, the Collection*, Durham, NC: Duke University Press, 1993.

Sutherland, Donald, *France 1789–1815, Revolution and Counterrevolution*, London: Fontana Press, 1985.

Tafuri, Manfredo, "Machine et Mémoire: The City in the Work of Le Corbusier", *Le Corbusier*, H Allen Brooks, ed., Princeton, NJ: Princeton University Press, 1987.

———, *Theories and History of Architecture*, New York: Granada, 1976.

———, *Venice and the Renaissance*, Jessica Levine trans., Cambridge, MA: MIT Press, 1995.

Talbot, William Henry Fox, "The Pencil of Nature: Brief historical sketch of the invention of the art", London: Longman & Co., 1844. Reprinted as "H Fox Talbot's The Pencil of Nature", anniversary facsimile, by Larry J Schaaf, Kraus, New York, 1989

Tschudi-Madsen, Stephan, *Restoration and Anti-Restoration*, Oslo: Universitetsforlaget, 1976.

Tuetey, Alexandre, and Jean Guiffrey, *La Commission du musée et la création du musée du Louvre*, Paris: Daupeley-Gouverneur, 1910.

Tuetey, Louis M, *Procès-verbaux de la commission temporaire des arts*, Paris: Librairie Ernest Leroux, 1912.

Turner, Paul Venable, *The Education of Le Corbusier: A Study of the Development of Le Corbusier's Thought 1900–1920*, New York: Garland, 1977.

Turtinen, Jan, *Världsarvets villkor: Intressen, förhandlingar och bruk i internationell politik*, Stockholm: Acta Universitatis Stockholmiensis, 2006.

Vidler, Anthony, *The Writing of the Walls: Architectural Theory in the Late Enlightenment*, Princeton NY: Princeton Architectural Press, 1987.

Vinegar, Aaron, "Viollet-le-Duc and Restoration in the Future Anterior", *Future Anterior*, Vol. III, No. 2, 2006, pp. 55–65.

Viollet-le-Duc, Eugène-Emmanuel, *Cités et ruines américaines: Mitla, Palenqué, Izamal, Chichen Itza, Uzmal*, Paris: 1863.

———, *Dictionnaire raisonné de l'architecture française du XIe au XVIe siècle*, Paris: B Bance and A Morel, 10 Vols., 1854–1868, 1867–1889. Hereafter referred to as *Dictionnaire*.

———, *The Foundations of Architecture: Selections from 'Dictionnaire raisonné'*, New York: Braziller, 1990.

———, *Histoire d'un dessinateur: Comment on apprend à dessiner*, (Translated as *Learning to Draw or the Story of a Young Designer*, New York: Putman, 1881), Paris: J Hetzel, 1879.

———, *Le Massif du Mont Blanc; Etude sur sa constitution géodésique et géologique sur les Transformations et sur l'état ancient et moderne de ses glaciers*, (Translated as *Mont Blanc, a Treatise*, B Bucknall trans., London: Sampson Low, Marston, Searle, and Rivington, 1877.), Paris: Libraire Polytechnique J Braudry, 1876.

———, "On Restoration", B Bucknall and Sampson Low trans., London: Marston, Low, and Searle, 1875. From the chapter "Restauration", in Viollet-le-Duc, Eugène-Emmanuel, Dictionnaire raisonné de l'architecture française du XIe au XVIe siècle, Paris: B Bance, A Morel, Vol. 8, 1866. Hereafter referred to as *On Restoration*.

Viollet-le-Duc, Eugène-Emmanuel, and Jean Baptiste Antoine Lassus, *Monographie de Notre-Dame de Paris et de la nouvelle sacristie*, Paris: (undated).

Walden, Russell, ed., *The Open Hand: Essays on Le Corbusier*, Cambridge, MA: MIT Press, 1977.

Wetterberg, Ola, *Monument och Miljö*, Göteborg: Chalmers Tekniska Högskola, 1992.

Wheeler, Michael, and Nigel Whiteley, eds., *The Lamp of Memory: Ruskin, Tradition and Architecture*, Manchester: Manchester University Press, 1992.

Witt, Inken, *Der moderne Denkmalkultus. Sein Wesen und seine Entstehung*, London: Architectural Association, 1997.

Wood, Christopher S, ed., *The Vienna School Reader: Politics and Art Historical Method in the 1930s*, New York: Zone Books, 2000.

Woodfield, Richard, ed., *Framing Formalism: Riegl's Work*, Amsterdam: G&B Arts International, 2001.

World Heritage 2002; *Shared legacy, common responsiblity*, Paris: World Heritage Centre, UNESCO, 2003.

Wright, Patrick, *On Living in an Old Country: The National Past In Contemporary Britain*, London: Verso, 1985.

Wrigley, Richard, "Breaking the Code: Interpreting French Revolutionary Iconoclasm", *Reflections on Revolution, Images of Romanticism*, Alison Yarrington and Kelvin Everest, eds., London: Routledge, 1993.

Wölfflin, Henrich, *Renaissance and Baroque*, Katherine Simon trans., Ithaca: Cornell University Press, 1964.

Young, James E, *The Texture of Memory: Holocaust Memorials and Meaning*, New Haven, CT: Yale University Press, 1993.

Zerner, Henri, "Alois Riegl: Art, Value, and Historicism", *Daedalus*, Vol. 105, 1976, pp. 177–178.

INDEX

ACKNOWLEDGEMENTS

The research for this book was carried out in the
context of my Ph.D., defended in December 2003 at the
KTH School of Architecture, Stockholm, but largely
written and conceived in the creative atmosphere
of the Histories and Theories programme of the
Architectural Association Graduate School, London,
in the period 1995–2000. To return to this material
after a time gap of over a decade has been an intriguing
and sometimes daunting experience. I have performed
a kind of archaeology of the thesis I put forward then,
tracing and sifting through archive material to reconstruct its central argument. My conclusion after
much digging was that it was best to leave most of
the texts intact, opting for a conservationist attitude
rather than one of modernisation. The undercurrent of
thought relates to the UK debate of the 1990s where,
specifically within the architectural discipline, the
role of conservation as an increasingly dominant and
regulatory practice affecting the built environment was
strongly debated and criticised. With the new 'lust' for
history in the postmodern discourse of the 1980s and
1990s, conservation was often framed as a reaction
against Modern Movement planning ideals. This
background led me to emphasis conservation's origin
in cultures of modernity, and its de-contextualising
aspects. In short, at that time I wanted to restore
conservation into the discourse of modernity, showing
its radical rather than conservative origins. Today,
when the heroic structures of the Modern Movement
themselves are heritage and the ideals that once
directed their creation are history, this in many senses
productive conflict is less present within architectural
discourse. Indeed, there is now a consensus around
the role of heritage in generating market value in
the form of identity, locality and sustainability, and
the conservation of the built environment is firmly
integrated into liberal planning policies in Europe
and beyond.

By taking a 'conservationist' attitude to my own argument,
an argument formulated in a debate that is at large already
fought, I hope however to convey the original passions and
complexities that once started this project and that have
driven it along: the rethinking of the binary opposition
between destruction and conservation; the spatial aspect
of conservation and the themes of displacement and
the museum.

I want to thank several people for helping me to bring
this project to a conclusion. Above all I want to thank
Tim Anstey for his editorial comments and his elegant
handling of my idiosyncratic English. Without Tim this
book would have turned out very differently in structure
and argumentation. I am deeply thankful for his
genourus commitment both intelectually and timewise.
I also want to thank Mark Cousins at the Architectural
Association, London, for his long-term support of
this work and Sven-Olov Wallenstein, Professor in
Philosophy, University of Södertörn, Stockholm who
supervised the final stages of the Ph.D. that forms the
foundation for the present text.

I am also indebted to my colleagues at the Oslo School
of Architecture and Design, not only for urging me to
publish this text and facilitating a sabbatical leave to
rewrite the manuscript, but also for their constant
intellectual input. In the creative context of the Oslo
Centre for Critical Architectural Studies I have been
able to discuss the work with Mari Lending and Mari
Hvattum but also with OCCAS' Ph.D. candidates,
specifically with Mattias Ekman and Lothar Diem both
of whom helped with the manuscript in generous and
productive ways. The Masters students in both my
design studio Re-Store and in AHO's Post-professional
Masters in Conservation have been exposed to
material from the book during the years and I'm
grateful for their comments. I have benefitted from
invitations to lecture on the work from colleagues
in several academic contexts: Fredric Bedoire, The
Conservation programme at Royal Institute of Art,
Stockholm; Dan Karlholm, School of Culture and
Communication, Södertörn University, Stockholm;
Mark Cousins, Graduate School, Architectural
Association; Theresa Stoppani, Architectural History
and Theory, University of Greenwich; Vaughan Hart,
Centre for Advanced Studies in Architecture, Bath
University; Eve Blau, Graduate School of Design,
Harvard University.

In this context I specially want to thank Mark Jarzombek
of the History, Theory and Criticism programme at MIT,
who acted as external reader of the PhD and Jorge
Otero-Pailos of GSAPP, Columbia University. Otero-
Pailos' invitation to publish part of the work in the
inaugural issue of *Future Anterior*, and later to be a guest

scholar at the Future Anterior Lab constructively lead to
the publication of the book.

I'm thankful for help with reference and illustration
material from the following libraries and archives:
the RIBA Library, the Warburg Institute Library and
the British Library, all in London; the Ruskin Library,
University of Lancaster, where I specially want to
thank Stephen Wildman for taking time to show me
Ruskin's daguerreotypes; Fondation Le Corbusier,
Musée Carnavalet and Musée du Louvre, all in Paris;
Kungliga Biblioteket, Vitterhetsakademiens Bibliotek,
Nordiska Museets Bibliotek and the library at the KTH
School of Architecture, Stockholm. My thanks also go
to Thomas Struth for allowing me to use his amazing
images in the present book.

Parts of this book have previously been published as
journal articles and I am thankful for their editors' help
in refining the arguments and texts. A shorter version
of chapter one was published in Swedish in *Agora:
journal for metafysisk spekulasjon*, Oslo, 2006. Part of
the second chapter was published in *Proceedings of
the Nordic Conference for Advanced Studies in Cultural
Studies*, Linköping University Electronic Press, 2005.
A shortened version of chapter three was published as
"The Cult of Age", in *Future Anterior, Journal of Historic
Preservation, History Theory and Criticism*, vol.1, no. 1,
2004. Extracts of this chapter have also been publish
in (theorising) *History in Architecture and Design,
Proceedings of the Nordic Journal of Architectural
Research*, Elizabeth Tostrup and Christian Hermansen
eds., Oslo 2003. The fourth chapter was originally
published as "Restoration in the Machine Age: Themes
of Conservation in Le Corbusier's Plan Voisin", in *AA-
Files*, 38, 1999.

I also want to thank Duncan McCorquodale at Black
Dog Publishing, who commissioned and edited the
book, and Alex Wright who designed it. Thanks to
you both for your thorough commitment as well as
your patience with the author's various delays and
hesitations. The publication of the book was generously
funded by the Norwegian Research Council.

Finally my thanks go to the two most precious, Disa and
Edgar, who through their entry into the world in 2001
and 2004 contributed, if not to conclude, certainly to
mature the argument of the book by making me shelve
it. These two little figures, evolving from small fragile
things to persons in their own right while this book
was written did not wait patiently for its conclusion
but insisted on its author's presence in their lives.
I thank them for that and this book is for them.

Thordis Arrhenius, Stockholm/Oslo March 2012

COLOPHON

Copyright 2012: Artifice Books on architecture, Black Dog Publishing, the author and artists.
Published by Artifice Books in association with Black Dog Publishing with the financial support of the Research Council of Norway

Artifice Books on architecture
10a Acton Street, London WC1X 9NG, United Kingdom

Tel: +44 (0)20 7713 5097
Fax: +44 (0)20 7713 8682
info@artificeonline.com
www.artificeonline.com

British Library Cataloguing-in-Publication Data.
A CIP record for this book is available from the British Library.

ISBN 978 1 907317 47 7

Artifice, London, UK, is an environmentally responsible company. *The Fragile Monument* is printed on FSC certified paper.